THE
M.I.N.D.S.E.T.
FRAMEWORK

REWIRE YOUR THINKING TO INSPIRE,
EMPOWER AND CULTIVATE A
HIGH PERFORMING TEAM

Sally Allen

The M.I.N.D.S.E.T. Framework / Allen, Sally. -- 1st ed.

ISBN: 978-1-997649-25-0

Acknowledgments

First, thank you to my husband Chris. You have patiently listened to my endless ideas, drafts, and late-night bursts of "this is brilliant" followed quickly by "this is terrible." Your support, love, and steady presence made this book possible, and your ability to smile through my caffeine-fueled ramblings deserves its own award.

To my family and friends, thank you for pretending to understand what I was talking about when I explained my chapters out loud. Your encouragement and occasional eye rolls kept me grounded.

To my clients, you inspired much of this book. Every conversation, challenge, and win we shared reminded me why this work matters. Thank you for trusting me, even when I used you as "anonymous examples."

And to the incredible community around me, thank you for cheering me on and for giving me stories, laughter, and perspective. This book is a reflection of all the people who poured into me, kept me laughing, and occasionally shoved snacks in my hand when I forgot to eat.

Dedication

To the leaders I have had the privilege of working with. Your courage and breakthroughs have been living proof that true, people-centered leadership is not theory, it is practical. You have taught me that the most powerful lessons are not written in textbooks but lived in the way we choose to lead others every day.

To the Reader

Thank you for choosing to read this book. I know there are countless books you could choose from, so it means a great deal that you are here. My hope is that what you read in these chapters gives you practical tools, new perspective, and encouragement for your own leadership journey. May these words remind you that growth is always possible and that the way you lead has the power to influence more than you realize. I am truly grateful you are here.

This book has taken hundreds of hours to write and rewrite. Draft after draft, edit after edit, and more than 40 hours of recording with corrections and retakes. I poured my heart into every page and every word you will hear. There were times when fatigue set in, when the setbacks felt endless, and when frustration brought a few tears, especially during the audio retakes. But each time I pressed on because I believe too deeply in what this message can unlock for leaders like you.

What you hold in your hands or hear in your ears is not just a book. It is resilience in written form. It is proof that mindset matters, not only as an idea but as a daily practice. It is the same practice I relied on to finish this project when doubt and exhaustion tried to take over. If it were easy, everyone would have done it. The fact that it was hard is exactly what makes it meaningful.

And if you are facing something hard right now, something that feels bigger than you, I want you to hear this: your mindset is your greatest tool. The thoughts you choose in the hardest moments will either hold you back or move you forward. The path may feel steep and the weight may feel crushing, but you can take the next step. And then the one after that. Keep climbing. Because when you reach the top, you will see that the very struggle you thought might break you became the very struggle that built you.

.

Table of Contents

What People Are Saying...1

Foreword..3

Introduction 5

    Section One: The Science...7

    Section Two: The Solution...7

    Section Three: The Success 8

Section 1: The Science 9

    Chapter 1: Does The Way You Think Really Matter?.............13

        What Is Mindset? 16

        The Biology Behind Mindset...22

        How Mindsets Are Formed 26

        Personal Experiences and Interpretations: The Stories We
Tell Ourselves...32

        Why Does It Matter?..34

        Mindset Reflection 37

    Chapter 2: Do You Truly Understand How Your Mind Works?...39

        Mindset and Self-Awareness 41

        Mindset and Limiting Beliefs 42

The Role of Core Values in Shaping Your Mindset 44

Building Habits That Align With Core Values.....................47

Mindset Reflection 49

Chapter 3: Leading Your Thoughts—Because Your Greatest
Challenge Is You..51

How Do I Start Leading My Thoughts?............................53

Mastering The Leader's Mindset 54

Mindset Reflection 58

Section 2: The Solution 59

Chapter 4: M—Move to Pause......................................63

Responding vs. Reacting..69

When to Pause? 70

How To Pause 71

Mindset Reflection 75

Chapter 5: I—Identify the Trigger...............................77

The Truth About Triggers 77

Why We Get Triggered..79

Recognize the Root Cause 80

The Many Faces of Triggers 81

When The Past Crashes Your Meeting.............................83

You Are Not Spiraling, You Are Just Hungry 84

How to Identify Your Triggers 85

Mindset Reflection 87

Chapter 6: N—Name the Thought...................................91

The Importance of Thought Labeling 92

Examples of Thought Labeling 95

Thought Labeling Exercises 101

Consider the Consequences of the Thought 103

Mindset Reflection 103

Chapter 7: D—Dissect the Belief.......................................107

Becoming a Detective..108

Core Beliefs vs Surface Thoughts 109

The Five "Whys" Method...111

The Friend Method 113

Putting it Together 115

Mindset Reflection 116

Chapter 8: S—Shift Your Perspective 119

Tools for Shifting Perspective..123

Gratitude as a Mindset Amplifier 128

Mindset Reflection 129

Chapter 9: E—Engage in Action..131

How Taking Action Rewires the Brain..............................132

How to Take the Right Kind of Action..............................134

Barriers to Action and How to Overcome Them 135

Fear of Failure or Judgment..136

How to Overcome It..137

Overwhelm or Lack of Clarity...138

How to Overcome It..138

Action Ideas to Consider 141

Mindset Reflection 143

Chapter 10: T—Track Your Progress.................................145

Why Tracking Progress is Crucial 146

When Something's Not Working.................................148

How to Track Progress.................................150

Mindset Reflection.................................153

Section 3: The Success 155

Chapter 11: Preparing for Setbacks 157

Understanding the Nature of Setbacks.................................158

Dealing With Setbacks 159

Mindset Reflection 161

Chapter 12: Continuous Implementation 163

Habit Formation and Reinforcement 165

The Role of Environment and Community.................................165

The Infinite Resilient Mindset.................................166

Mindset Reflection 167

Conclusion.................................169

The M.I.N.D.S.E.T. Framework: Your Recap.................................171

About the Author, Sally Allen.................................173

References 175

What People Are Saying

Working with Sally as my coach during my transition into executive leadership has been transformative. This book captures the same mindset she taught me, practical framework to pause, shift perspective, and lead with clarity that strengthened both my confidence and my team's resilience. It's a resource I can reference and share with others, and I highly recommend it to any leader looking to elevate their impact.

Nani Binder, Vice President, Inflight, Allegiant

Sally Allen's book MINDSET Framework is an impressive piece of work. Short and sweet, her book helps one unlock how to stop holding yourself back! She shares a powerful action-oriented guide on how to reframe one's state of mind working from a clinical foundation on how we are wired. Sally in the book builds on that key background and takes it forward with the more important steps that translate awareness and understanding into gamechanger actions — straightforward playbook that executives, business owners and leaders will use regularly and share with others.

Dr. Bo Charles Abiodun, Senior Vice President

Sally Allen's The M.I.N.D.S.E.T. Framework is a rare blend of neuroscience, storytelling, and practical leadership tools. It's honest, inspiring, and deeply actionable — a must-read for anyone who wants to shift from surviving to thriving and lead with clarity, resilience, and courage.

Gianna Driver, Chief People Officer

This book is a powerful blend of research-backed insight and practical tools. Sally's framework makes mindset shifts feel not only possible but, personally authentic and actionable. A must-read for anyone serious about growth.

Lauren Bates, President & Board Chair

Foreword

When I first met Sally Allen, I was struck not only by her wisdom but also by her presence. She carries both strength and gentleness; she's the kind of leader who doesn't just speak about resilience, but embodies it. Reading The M.I.N.D.S.E.T. Framework feels like sitting across from her, hearing both her hard-won lessons and her hopeful encouragement.

This book is not another leadership manual filled with jargon and quick fixes. It is Sally's generous offering of truth, science, and lived experience. She takes us into the depths of her own story, with moments of struggle, survival, and courage, and then lifts us up with practical, actionable tools. What makes her work so powerful is this combination: it's as raw as it is rigorous, as human as it is strategic.

Sally's story reminds us that while we don't choose the circumstances we're born into, we do choose how we respond. Her life's work is a testament to the fact that no matter our beginnings, we can rise, rewire, and create change not only for ourselves but for those we lead.

Leaders at every level will find themselves here. Whether you're navigating team challenges, managing constant change, or confronting your own inner critic, Sally provides a roadmap for rewiring thought patterns in ways that create clarity, resilience, and authentic connection. The M.I.N.D.S.E.T. framework is not just theory; it's a practice that can help you pause, reframe, act with intention, and ultimately lead yourself and others with more courage and compassion.

Most of all, this book is an invitation. An invitation to stop surviving and start thriving. To step away from rigid patterns that keep us small and embrace the resilient mindset that allows us—and those we lead—to grow.

It's a privilege to introduce Sally's work to you. I know that if you lean into these pages, you'll not only discover new ways of thinking, but new ways of living and leading.

— Gianna Driver, Menlo Park, California

Introduction

Most little girls wish for ponies or princess dresses when they turn eight.

I wished I could die.

Not exactly the mindset you'd expect from a child, right? But that was my reality. While other kids were dreaming about fairy tales, I was just trying to escape a life that felt like a nightmare.

Now, I know that's a heavy way to start a book, but hang in there with me. Because what I'm about to share isn't a story about staying stuck in pain. It's about rising from it. It's about transformation. And it's about the truth that your mindset, yes, yours, has the power to change everything.

Here's the thing: Getting from a place of hopelessness to the life I live today didn't happen because I thought happy thoughts or stuck a vision board on my fridge. In fact, most of the "just change your mindset" advice I came across felt about as helpful as a bucket full of holes. Uplifting on the surface, but absolutely useless when life was leaking through every crack.

My first real mindset shift didn't happen during my childhood. It didn't come from a book, a quote, or a feel-good seminar. It happened when I was 24 years old, on the floor, being strangled. My four-year-old son, my baby, had just been thrown across the room after trying to save me. That detail still rips my heart open. In his innocence and bravery, he did what no child should ever have to do.

He ran toward danger for his mom.

And in that terrifying, heartbreaking moment, something inside me snapped into place. A light bulb went off. Not the motivational quote kind. The raw, soul-deep kind. It was the moment I knew, if I didn't change, everything would stay broken. I wasn't just trying to survive. I was trying to rewrite the future for both of us. I realized I couldn't wait for someone to save me. I couldn't keep living in a victim mentality and expect anything to change. I had to choose a different path. I had to think differently to act differently.

That's when my real mindset journey began.

It wasn't about pretending everything was okay. It was about understanding that the only way forward was through intentional mental shifts. I began to grasp that mindset wasn't just a concept, it was the key to action, and if I wanted to create a different life, it had to start in my mind first.

The tools I'll be sharing with you in this book aren't fluff; they're the exact strategies that helped me shift from surviving to thriving. They've changed my life, and I've seen them transform the lives of countless clients who were ready to flip the switch. These are *proven principles* that work, as long as you're willing to do the work.

That's why I wrote this book, not to give you false hope or a list of buzzwords that sound good on Instagram but don't hold up in real life. This isn't a get-rich-quick scheme. It's not about pretending hard enough until your problems vanish. This book is a *tool*, and just like any tool, its power depends on if and how you use it.

So, here's your official invitation: Don't just read this book. Live it. Whether you're a business owner, a CEO, an emerging leader, or a mom trying to hold it all together, this book is for you. These mindset shifts aren't just theory; they're tools. They're how you get back up, how you move forward, and how you lead yourself through whatever you're facing.

Your story might look nothing like mine, and that's okay. Maybe you had a loving childhood, maybe you didn't. Maybe you're successful on paper but quietly struggling, or maybe you're just tired of pushing so hard and still feeling stuck. Wherever you are, your mindset is playing a huge role.

This book will help you figure out what that role is and how to shift it.

Let me be clear: I can't promise you ease. True growth never comes wrapped in comfort. But I can promise you this: It's worth it. The life waiting for you on the other side of a rewired mindset is fuller, freer, and far more powerful than anything fear or doubt ever offered you.

Imagine having the tools to help you master your mindset so that no one could hijack your peace or give you a reason to overthink. You wouldn't need to second-guess yourself, seek constant validation, or spin in mental loops after one tough conversation. You'd lead with clarity, recover faster, and trust your own voice no matter what room you walk into. That's not a pipe dream. That's what a rewired mindset looks like.

So, how does this book work? Let me break it down for you:

Section One: The Science.

I know, I know. The word "science" might make you want to skip ahead, but trust me, this isn't a textbook. Think of it as the foundation. The toolbox, if you will. You don't need to memorize anything or pass a test, but having a basic understanding of how the brain works will give you a solid starting point for real, lasting change.

Section Two: The Solution.

Here's where we put tools *in* the toolbox. I'll walk you through my signature MINDSET framework (yes, it's an acronym, and a good one, if I may say so). This is where the magic happens. You'll get practical strategies to rewire the way you think, lead, and live.

Section Three: The Success

You've got the tools, and you understand the science, but let's be honest, most self-help books fall flat right here. That's why this section is your manual for implementation. Because changing your mindset isn't a one-time event, it's a daily decision. This final section is your guide for sustaining the transformation.

And don't worry, I'll be right here with you the whole way. No judgment, no perfectionism, and yes, the occasional laugh (because if we can't laugh at ourselves while growing, what's the point?).

So, before we dive in, take a breath. Roll your shoulders back, silence the notifications, and give yourself permission to be fully present.

This is your time. Let's flip the switch from merely surviving to truly thriving.

Section 1: The Science

Have you ever questioned the state of your mind and how it got there? Let me tell you about one of my clients. We'll call him John to protect his privacy.

John is a senior leader at a fast-paced company. Smart, respected, and juggling more than most people can imagine. But when we started working together, he was completely burnt out.

After a long day, John would get home, collapse on the couch, and scroll on his phone while the kids screamed in the background. He'd tell himself, "I should go to the gym... I should spend time with the kids... I should be more present..." But instead, he sat there, exhausted. His wife was juggling dinner and trying to keep the household running, but he didn't have the energy to engage. He wasn't lazy; he was depleted, and deep down, he hated that this had become his default. Each night ended the same way: guilt, disappointment, and a restless night of sleep.

"Why am I like this?" he asked me. "Why can't I just get it together?"

Here's the thing: John didn't have a discipline problem. He had a *direction* problem. His mindset was stuck like a GPS that kept recalculating but never actually moving the car forward. Through one of the frameworks in this book, John began to see the pattern. His brain wasn't sabotaging him on purpose; it was just running a familiar program. He'd created mental shortcuts based on stress, exhaustion, and default behaviors, and over time, those shortcuts became deeply worn grooves.

To get out of it, we started with three foundational mindset questions:

1. Does the way you think really matter?

2. Do you truly understand how your mind works?

3. Are you intentionally leading your mind or letting it lead you?

I hear this all the time from my clients: "How do I shift my mindset? Why do I keep falling into the same cycles? What's wrong with me?"

Nothing's wrong with you.

Your brain is just doing what it's been trained to do, sticking to what it knows, even if what it knows is making you miserable. It's like your mind got stuck in one lane and keeps replaying the same tired soundtrack, hoping something changes. But spoiler alert: nothing changes if nothing changes.

Most people aren't lazy. They often just don't know how to interrupt and break the cycle. They don't need more pressure, they need clarity and tools. And that starts with learning how to lead your mind instead of being led by it.

The three powerful questions above create the foundation for understanding and ultimately rewiring your mindset. I mean, you won't bother changing your mindset if you don't actually believe your thoughts matter, right? That's like trying to clean out your closet without admitting you might be a bit of a shoe hoarder.

And how can you change your mindset if you don't even know your thoughts or the patterns they're sneaking around in? More importantly, how can you rewire your brain if you're not even sure where the current wiring is taking you? Because it might be leading you straight into a mental traffic jam where the same old thoughts just keep circling the block, getting nowhere.

By answering these three questions and looking at the science of mindset, you'll start to see the golden thread tying all of these ideas together. That's exactly what section one of this book is about.

Now, don't worry, this isn't some dusty college lecture where we'll memorize brain anatomy and call it a day. Yes, we'll get into some neuroscience, but always through the lens of *understanding* your mind so you can actually *change* it.

Why does it matter to get these foundations down before jumping to solutions? Same reason you don't just toss ingredients into a bowl and hope for a cake. You need the right measurements, the right order, and the right temperature, or you'll end up with a collapsed mess that doesn't even resemble what you were aiming for. Mindset works the same way. If you skip the foundational work, no solution will stick. You have to start with the right ingredients if you want the recipe to turn out right.

So. Deep breath. Let's do this.

Chapter 1

Does The Way You Think Really Matter?

Your leadership will never outgrow your mindset.
Expand your thinking, and everything else will rise to meet it.

–Sally Allen

There's one question that sits at the core of this entire journey. Without it, none of the rewiring matters. Why? Because if your thinking doesn't actually shape your life, then what's the point of trying to change it? That's why this question isn't just important. It's the spark that ignites transformation.

As I mentioned earlier, I was 24 years old when that first mindset shift hit me during one of the darkest moments of my life. It wasn't planned. It wasn't pretty. But it was crystal clear. Lying on that floor, gasping for air, something inside me said, "You've given up on life... but what about your little boy? Should your four-year-old son be the one saving you? Or should you be the one protecting him?"

Until then, I hadn't realized how deeply I'd been stuck in a victim mentality. Now, to be fair, I had every reason to feel that way. Up until that moment, victimhood was all I had ever known. Abuse. Oppression. Survival. That was my normal. But this was my wake-up call. For the first time, I could see the bigger picture. Yes, life had been unfair. Yes, I had been hurt. But I didn't have to stay stuck in that story.

That moment didn't just shake me. It forced a decision. Two, actually. First, I would never let my son be in that position again. I would protect him with everything I had. Second, I had to run. Not emotionally. Not symbolically. I mean I physically ran. I grabbed my little boy and got out. That was the beginning of the real work. The moment mindset stopped being a buzzword and became a lifeline. These were my first resilient thoughts, the first time I intentionally started to shift my mindset. Not perfectly. Not instantly. But on purpose.

It didn't end there. That was just the beginning. Over time, I started to see how that same victim mindset shows up everywhere—not just in personal survival, but in leadership too. I've seen it play out over and over again. Leaders with incredible potential, stuck in limited thinking and focused on what's working against them instead of what's already within reach: resources, relationships, and opportunities. All right there, but blocked by old beliefs. Let me paint the picture for you.

One of the leaders I worked with (let's call her Marissa) was in a middle management role, responsible for leading a team of five. When we first started working together, Marissa felt stuck. Her team had developed a reputation for underperforming. They consistently missed deadlines, morale was low, and no matter what she tried, nothing seemed to move the needle. From her perspective, the reasons were obvious: one team member talked too much and distracted the others, they had the oldest computers in the office that froze like clockwork, and they always got the most difficult clients, clearly, she thought, because upper management didn't like her.

In her mind, they were set up to fail, and while she never said it out loud, she quietly hoped for a transfer to a team with fewer landmines. What Marissa didn't realize was how profoundly her thought patterns were driving her leadership behaviors. Her internal beliefs about her team, her company, and herself leaked into everything: how she communicated, how she made decisions, and how she showed up when things went sideways. She grew passive in meetings, dismissive of new ideas, and reactive with her team. Her tone and body language screamed what her words didn't: "This isn't fixable, so don't bother trying." And here's the thing about leadership energy: it's contagious. Without even meaning to, Marissa had become the thermostat, not the thermometer. Her team picked up on her resignation, and they internalized it. They stopped stretching, stopped sharing, and started aiming for the bare minimum just to make it through the day without conflict. The bar dropped and the culture settled underneath it.

From the outside, the root cause seems obvious, but when you're in the thick of it like Marissa was, it's nearly impossible to see that the biggest limitation isn't the equipment, the clients, or even the team. It's the leader's thinking behind the wheel. For Marissa, the turning point came from the foundational mindset questions:

1. Does the way you think really matter?

2. Do you understand how your mind actually works?

3. Are you intentionally leading your mind or is it running the show unchecked?

I'm repeating these questions because of how important they are. They didn't just spark insight; they interrupted the narrative. She realized her thoughts weren't neutral; they were directional. They were guiding her posture, her presence, and her performance, and for the first time, she could name the truth: The obstacle wasn't external. It was her mindset in the driver's seat.

That realization was the beginning of real change.

What Is Mindset?

The Merriam-Webster dictionary defines mindset as "a mental attitude" or "a rigid state of mind." Cute. But let's be real, that sounds like it was written before Wi-Fi and emotional intelligence existed. A little old. A little quaint. Very paper dictionary energy. In reality, mindset isn't just a one-off belief or a passing opinion. It's a constant internal commentary that shapes how you interpret the world, and more importantly, how you operate within it. Think of it like the filter on your favorite photo app. Same scene, different vibe. Two people can experience the exact same moment, but depending on their mental filter, one sees challenge and opportunity while the other sees stress and shutdown. The moment doesn't change, the mindset does. That's what makes it powerful, and that's what makes it modern. This isn't self-help fluff. This is how people function, lead, and live in real time. Mindset is how you make sense of the world and yourself. It influences not only how you think, but how you feel and behave in nearly every situation especially when stakes are high. And if you're in leadership, it's not just influencing you, it's setting the tone for everyone you lead.

Let me illustrate this with a story you've probably seen unfold in your own workplace, and maybe even in your own head.

Two candidates are in final consideration for a high-level role. Their résumés are nearly identical. They have the same qualifications, the same achievements, and the same ambition. Each receives a call from the hiring manager with the same message: "You've made it to the final round. As a final step, we're assigning a critical, high-pressure project. It's due in 24 hours."

Now the real test begins.

Candidate One leaves the interview feeling defeated. "They've set me up to fail," he tells himself. "There's no way to pull this off in one day." That evening, instead of starting the project, he writes a long, detailed explanation of why the assignment is unrealistic. He brings up industry standards, personal values, and why this kind of evaluation feels unfair. It feels honest. It feels cathartic. But it's not the assignment.

Candidate Two walks out with eyebrows raised but focus intact. "This is intense," she tells herself. "But if they asked me to do it, they must believe I can handle it." She doesn't question the fairness. She doesn't try to read between the lines. She just gets to work. She sketches out ideas, reaches out to a few trusted voices, and spends the evening building the best solution she can. It's not flawless, but it's real. It shows leadership, initiative, and follow-through.

The next morning, Candidate One turns in a critique. Candidate Two turns in a solution.

Now ask yourself: Who gets the job?

The key difference here isn't skill, education, or even how much sleep they got the night before. It's mindset. One defaulted to what we call a **rigid mindset**, where obstacles are viewed as evidence of unfairness or inadequacy. The other leaned into a **resilient mindset**, where challenges are approached with adaptability, creativity, and belief in growth.

This distinction has roots in the research of **Dr. Carol Dweck**, a Stanford psychologist whose work on fixed and growth mindsets has reshaped how we understand potential. In her studies, Dweck found that people with a fixed mindset believe their intelligence and talents are set in stone—what you're born with is what you've got. In contrast, those with a growth mindset believe that effort, learning, and perseverance can expand their capabilities.

For this book, we're using the terms **rigid** and **resilient** not just because they sound catchy, but because they capture two fundamentally different leadership mindsets. A rigid mindset cracks under pressure. It interprets setbacks as personal failures and gets stuck in survival mode. It resists change, clings to control, and avoids risk. A resilient mindset, by definition, is the capacity to recover quickly from difficulties. In leadership, that means being able to bend without breaking. Resilient leaders adapt. They learn, recalibrate, and keep showing up even when the path forward isn't clear. They don't just survive pressure. They grow through it. And in today's ever-changing landscape, resilience is no longer optional. It is a competitive advantage.

In leadership, what matters most isn't whether you get knocked down. Let's be honest, you will. That's part of the deal. The real question is whether you have the mindset to get back up. Can you recover mentally? Can you reframe the setback, re-engage your focus, and recommit to forward momentum? Rigid leaders spiral. Resilient leaders reset.

The difference isn't toughness, it's mental flexibility, and that's not some soft-skill buzzword. It's a research-backed capability tied to improved problem-solving, emotional regulation, and long-term performance outcomes. The best leaders aren't the ones who avoid stress. They're the ones whose mindset is trained to handle it and rise stronger every time.

And this isn't just feel-good philosophy, it's backed by science.

Psychologists **Dr. Richard Lazarus** and **Dr. Susan Folkman** developed what's known as **Cognitive Appraisal Theory**, a powerful framework that shows it's not the event itself that causes stress it's how we interpret it (1984). In one of their studies, participants were placed in a high-pressure scenario. Half were told it was a *threat* while the other half were told it was a *challenge*. That single difference in framing drastically affected performance. The threat group became anxious, mentally exhausted, and overwhelmed. The challenge group stayed focused, motivated, and resourceful.

Same event. Different narrative. Wildly different outcome.

What does that tell us? That perception drives response. And perception is always shaped by mindset. In leadership, this isn't a minor detail. It's the whole game.

When a leader operates from a rigid mindset, they tend to interpret problems as personal attacks, treat constraints as dead ends, and lead with defensiveness. Their team quickly picks up on the vibe. Ideas shrink, innovation dies, and people stop speaking up. Over time, you don't just have low performance, you have a culture of fear wearing a badge that says "professionalism."

But a resilient mindset? That's a different story.

A resilient leader interprets setbacks as signals, not stop signs. They stay curious. They stay open. They ask better questions instead of assigning blame. And in doing so, they give their team psychological permission to stretch, to fail forward, and to grow. That mindset becomes the emotional climate others operate in. Your thinking literally becomes your team's oxygen.

Here's the leadership truth most people don't tell you: **Your mindset is never just yours**. It's contagious, it multiplies, and over time, it shapes not just how you lead but how others rise under your leadership. So, next time you're handed a metaphorical 24-hour project that feels impossible, pause and ask yourself: Is this the beginning of my exit story or my breakthrough? Because the answer has less to do with your to-do list and everything to do with your mindset.

Here are a few examples of rigid vs resilient thinking:

Rigid Mindset	Resilient Mindset
My value comes from being busy. If I slow down, I'm falling behind. Rest feels like laziness. I equate constant motion with worth.	Rest is a leadership skill. My clarity improves when I create room to think. I prioritize recovery because burnout serves no one.
If I don't have all the answers, I lose credibility. Admitting uncertainty feels like weakness, so I stay silent or fake confidence.	I don't need to have all the answers. I need to ask the right questions. I lead with curiosity and invite collaboration.
Delegating feels like weakness. I should be able to handle it all myself. Asking for help feels like failure, so I take it all on, even when it's too much.	I focus on what I can influence and stay grounded when things shift. Control isn't the goal—clarity and adaptability are.
I can't trust others to do it right, so I have to stay in the weeds. Letting go feels risky, so I stay stuck in the details instead of leading.	Empowering others to take ownership builds stronger, more resilient teams. Trust isn't optional. It's the foundation of sustainable leadership.
Mistakes reflect poorly on me, so I avoid risks. If there's a chance I'll mess up, I'd rather not try at all. Playing it safe feels more secure than putting myself on the line.	Mistakes are part of progress. I use them to refine, not retreat. Every misstep is feedback. I don't fear failure. I use it to sharpen my approach and move forward with more clarity.

When we compare the two, I think it's pretty clear which side of the mindset fence we want to be on. Resilient? Yes, please! Sign us up for the flexible, adaptive, growth-oriented version of ourselves. But here's the catch: Where we *want* to be and where we *are* aren't always the same zip code. Most of us aren't operating from a resilient mindset 24/7. We're reacting, protecting, and occasionally bracing for impact like it's our full-time job.

Objectively, it's obvious that a resilient mindset makes for stronger leaders, more creative problem solvers, and better humans overall. But mindset isn't shaped in a vacuum. It's influenced by dozens of variables: early experiences, past failures, cultural messaging, stress levels, sleep (or lack thereof), and whether or not you had to deal with Greg from accounting before your coffee kicked in.

So, if you've just read through the comparison of rigid and resilient mindsets and thought, "Yikes... I think I might be living rent free in Rigidville," don't panic. Don't close the book. Don't decide that mindset mastery is for other people who do sunrise journaling and green smoothies. That's the beautiful part of this entire journey: **Mindsets are malleable**.

You are not cement. You are clay.

Let me say it plainly: If you currently lean toward a rigid mindset, be encouraged. I'm not here to judge you, I'm here to remind you that change is not only possible, it's probable when you're intentional. I've seen countless professionals shift from rigid to resilient leaders. They used to play it safe, but now they're taking bold, strategic risks. They saw feedback as an attack, and now they're using it as rocket fuel for growth. And I'm not talking about surface-level change where people slap on a smile and pretend everything's fine. I'm talking about deep, internal rewiring—the kind of transformation that doesn't just change how you show up at work, but how you show up in your life.

My own mindset? It wasn't always what it is now. I've lived on both sides of the equation. I've battled the inner critic, clung to certainty, and resisted change like it was a full time sport. But the shift came not all at once, but through small, intentional steps that added up over time. It wasn't magic, it was mindset work, and if I can do it, so can you.

So, take heart. A rigid mindset is not a life sentence. It's just a snapshot, a moment in your story, not the whole narrative. And if you're willing to get curious instead of judgmental and to engage rather than retreat, then this chapter of your life can be the turning point. The mindset you have today doesn't have to be the mindset you lead with tomorrow.

But before we dive into the *how* of change, let's first look at *why* it's possible. That starts with the biology behind your mindset. Understanding the brain isn't just for neuroscientists and TED Talk junkies; it's the foundation for rewiring the very thoughts that have been quietly steering your leadership.

Let's take a peek under the hood.

The Biology Behind Mindset

I remember my first day of kindergarten. While most kids were buzzing with excitement, clinging to their backpacks and waving goodbye to their parents, I was quietly taking it all in like a tiny five-year-old analyst assessing the chaos. The day passed, and when the final bell rang, I walked outside with the rest of the class, expecting someone to be there waiting for me.

One by one, kids were scooped up laughing, hugging, skipping off hand in hand like a Hallmark commercial. But I just stood there. Watching. Waiting.

No one came.

I had no idea where to go or how to get home, but I knew I had to do something. *(Side note: this was in Guyana, where it was perfectly normal for kids to walk home from school, but not on day one, in a storm, alone.)* It was pouring rain as I ran down the street, desperately searching for anything familiar. At last, I found a landmark I recognized: an old, scary looking bridge that looked like it belonged in a Brothers Grimm story. Since I couldn't swim, I was already terrified of water and with the downpour that day, the river was raging like it had something to prove.

I was terrified as I crawled across the bridge, certain I was going to fall in and drown (which, by the way, I almost did). By some miracle, I made it home in one piece, soaking wet, traumatized, and more afraid of water than ever.

Fast forward a few decades and I'm an adult, living a beautiful life in America, married to a wonderful husband... and still deeply afraid of water. The twist? I also love it. I love being near it. I love the sound, the peace, the beauty of it all but I wouldn't go in past my waist. The fear had a grip on me, even while the water kept calling to me.

Eventually, I got tired of being scared. Tired of being a grown woman, leading a perfectly rational life, while holding onto a fear that made absolutely no sense anymore. So, I decided to face it. I signed up for swim lessons as the **only adult** in the class. Yep. Surrounded by fearless toddlers doing cannonballs while I practiced blowing bubbles like a nervous sea otter.

It was embarrassing, physically exhausting, and mentally brutal. Flashbacks from that rainy bridge day hit hard, but I pushed through, week after week, inch by inch, until I finally learned how to swim.

So what changed? What flipped the script from *never* to *now*? What actually rewired my brain? It's a magical thing called **neuroplasticity** and it's one of the most powerful forces behind every mindset shift.

Neuroplasticity

Put very simply, neuroplasticity is your brain's ability to change, rewire, and adapt over time. Think of it as your brain's built in upgrade system minus the annoying software prompts. The human brain is incredibly malleable, thanks to neurons—tiny messengers that act as the building blocks of everything you think, feel, and do. These neurons are constantly firing, forming new connections, and responding to whatever signals you send them, whether those signals are helpful or not.

Here's the good news: Your brain can literally change based on how you think, what you focus on, and what you practice consistently. Neuroplasticity allows your brain to reorganize existing pathways, create new connections, and yes, in some cases even grow brand new neurons. (Turns out, your brain didn't stop developing the day you graduated high school.)

That means something powerful: **You are not stuck**. Your mindset isn't hardwired. You're not doomed to think the way you've always thought or react the way you've always reacted. With intention, repetition, and the right tools, you can train your brain to support a mindset that works *for* you not against you.

So if you've ever said, "I'm just not wired for this," I've got great news: You can **re**wire.

Let me give you a visual. Picture your brain as an open field covered in knee high grass and wildflowers. Every choice you make or thought you repeat is like walking through that field trampling a path as you go. The more often you take the same route, the more defined that path becomes. Eventually, it's automatic. You go that way without even thinking. Your mindset is really just a well-worn set of those paths—reinforced beliefs, habitual reactions, and go-to interpretations.

Now here's the powerful part: When you choose a new thought or behavior, something different from your norm, it's like stepping off the old trail and carving a new one. It'll feel awkward at first. Unnatural even. You'll want to default back to the comfortable route, but with repetition and intention, that new path starts to take shape, and one day, it becomes the new normal.

In my own story, my default mental path around water was pure fear and avoidance. Water equaled danger. Period. That belief got stronger every time I reinforced it with more avoidance. My brain wasn't being dramatic, it was doing its job. Keeping me alive. Keeping me "safe."

That instinct comes from deep inside the brain, specifically, the **amygdala**. It's part of the limbic system and it's basically the brain's personal bodyguard. It scans constantly for potential threats and kicks in our survival response when it senses danger. This is what activates the well known "fight, flight, or freeze" response.

Here's the catch: The amygdala doesn't fact check. It doesn't ask, "Is this truly dangerous?" It just reacts. If something has been associated with fear, pain, or discomfort (hello, childhood bridge story) the amygdala files it under *Avoid Forever* and keeps triggering the alarm bells any time you go near it.

So when I signed up for adult swim lessons, my brain protested like a toddler in a toy aisle. It felt unfamiliar, risky, and embarrassing. I almost canceled three times. From my brain's perspective, staying away from water was the better bet. That was the "safe" thing to do.

But here's what I've learned: **safety and growth don't always share a room.**

The moment I chose to show up scared, unsure, but willing, I started to build a new neural pathway. A new message began to emerge: *This is safe. This is okay. You can do this.* And every time I practiced, that message got a little stronger. With enough repetition, the fearful association lost power. The new path of confidence and calm became my default. That's neuroplasticity in action. Not abstract theory. Not just neuroscience jargon. But actual, life-changing biology doing what it does best: **adapting**. And if my brain can rewrite decades of fear to create a new relationship with water, imagine what your brain can do with a little direction, consistency, and willingness to walk a new path.

That's neuroplasticity.

It's the reason I can now enjoy long walks on the beach with my dogs and spend hours in the pool with my family without panic and without feeling like I'm auditioning for a survival episode. That's neuroplasticity in action.

It's what allows us to unlearn fear, rewrite outdated stories, and build new mental frameworks that actually support the life we want to live.

This isn't about slapping on a positive affirmation and hoping for the best. It's science, and one of the most powerful tools we have when it comes to changing our mindset. Not just for confidence, but for leadership, growth, parenting, performance, and everyday decision making.

Here's the truth: Changing your mind isn't just "thinking differently." That's the surface level. The real transformation happens when you train your brain to *respond* differently. You're not just shifting thoughts, you're creating new patterns, new beliefs, and new default settings. You're reconditioning the system. And like any system, your brain needs clear inputs. It needs practice, repetition, and support. But once it gets the message, it adapts. That's the gift. The same mind that once protected you through fear can evolve to empower you through courage.

So, the next time someone says, "You've changed," take it as a compliment, because, yes, you have! And it's not just personal growth. It's neurological growth. Which, in case you're wondering, is far more impressive than that 6 AM bootcamp you skipped last Tuesday.

How Mindsets Are Formed

Let's talk about the ancient brain in a modern world.

To understand why our mindset can so easily default to fear, self-protection, and worst-case scenario thinking, we need to look back into the past. (A few thousand years back, actually!) Our ancestors weren't worried about performance reviews or inbox overload. They were worried about staying alive. Life was quite literally a survival game. Humans lived in caves or open terrain, constantly on alert for physical threats from wild animals, natural disasters, and hostile tribes. The brain evolved under pressure, wired to notice danger faster than safety, and to react quickly in order to avoid death.

As anthropologist Alan Goodman explains, "It's an ancient mammalian system adapted to protect hunter-gatherers" (Novak. 2021). The same fight-or-flight response that once helped our ancestors survive wild predators now gets triggered by deadlines, emails, and awkward meetings. What kept us alive in caves is still running in the background—only now, it often works against us.

That's where the fight, flight, or freeze response originated. If you were being chased by a lion, you didn't have time to pause and journal about your feelings or assess all possible outcomes. You needed to react instantly. And the people who *didn't*? Well, they didn't live long enough to pass on their wisdom or their genes.

This survival first mindset was incredibly effective… back then.

Here's the thing: Evolution hasn't caught up to modern life. Our brains haven't had enough time to adapt to a world where lions don't lurk outside the office. We don't need to run for our lives on a daily basis, but our brain still behaves as if we do.

There's research to back this up. **Dr. Joseph LeDoux**, a neuroscientist at New York University, has spent decades studying how the brain processes fear (1998). His work shows that the amygdala reacts *before* the thinking part of the brain (the prefrontal cortex) even has time to assess whether there's an actual threat. In other words, your brain is programmed to protect you *first*, and ask questions *later*.

This explains why we can interpret a tough email from our boss or a disappointing comment from a colleague as a full blown threat. Our brain doesn't know the difference between a lion and a leadership challenge. It just senses discomfort, uncertainty, or rejection and it hits the panic button.

So, what does this mean for mindset? It means that many of our thought patterns are **inherited defaults** passed down through generations of survival-focused humans. Our brains are still running ancient software in a modern world, and without intentional rewiring, we're more likely to live in defense mode, overreacting, avoiding risk, and reinforcing beliefs that keep us small—all under the illusion of staying "safe."

But here's the good news: We no longer live in caves. Most of us aren't dodging lions. And thanks to the incredible power of neuroplasticity, we don't have to be ruled by fear based thinking anymore. We can train the brain to recognize the difference between real danger and everyday discomfort. We can develop a mindset that leads rather than reacts, that grows rather than defends. But first, we have to understand what we're working with and why our ancient brain sometimes behaves like it's still crouched in a cave.

Childhood: The Original Operating System.

Before you ever led a team, sent your first email, or sat in a boardroom, you were shaped by something far more foundational: childhood.

Whether we like it or not, the way we were raised creates the first version of our mindset. It's the original operating system downloaded in the background while we were just trying to survive elementary school and figure out how Velcro shoes worked. Every message we received, explicit or implied, formed beliefs about who we were, what we could do, and how the world worked. And here's something important: Developing a rigid mindset doesn't automatically mean you had bad parents. I've worked with many high-performing professionals who grew up in loving homes, and yet still struggle with limiting beliefs that trace all the way back to something seemingly small, like a misunderstood comment or a sarcastic remark taken to heart at age six.

Kids don't process things the way adults do. They're not emotionally sophisticated, they're *spongy*. And what seems minor to us now could've landed like a thunderclap back then. For example, maybe you were praised constantly for being "smart," but the first time you struggled with something, you panicked because smart people shouldn't struggle, right?

Or maybe you were told you were "bad at math" once in third grade, and thirty years later, you're still avoiding spreadsheets like they're contagious.

I've seen it happen over and over again: A leader in the workplace unknowingly processing a situation through the lens of a seven-year-old child who felt like they weren't enough. Let's take little Sarah, for instance. She loved to run. She was fast, confident, and loved the thrill of competing. Her parents often praised her for being "the fastest," and Sarah associated that praise with her worth. Then one day, she tripped mid race, got up, and still placed third. She was proud of herself until she heard her dad yell, "It's unfair! Someone tripped her!"

He meant well. He wanted to protect her. But that moment created a new belief in Sarah's mind: *If I fall, I won't be praised. If I'm not the best, something must be wrong.* Fast forward a few years, and Sarah becomes someone who avoids challenges she might fail at and blames others when things don't go her way, not because she's a bad person, but because her brain is running a mindset built for approval, not growth.

It's not just about Sarah. It's all of us. The beliefs we form in childhood don't stay neatly tucked away in our past. They come with us into relationships, into careers, into leadership, and if we're not aware of them, they end up leading the show from behind the scenes.

Here's what the research says: When children are praised for effort, they're more likely to develop a resilient mindset. They learn that they can improve with time and practice. But when they're only praised for outcomes like being "smart" or "the best," they start to believe that their value lies in perfection, and anything less than that becomes a threat to their identity.

Even well intended correction can create fear. A parent who sharply criticizes mistakes may believe they're pushing for excellence, but a child might internalize that failure equals rejection. And what do kids do when they fear rejection? They play it safe. They stay small. They avoid anything that carries risk.

Sound familiar?

Now imagine those same kids, but now as adults leading teams, running businesses, navigating pressure, and trying to make bold decisions. They're still operating through a filter built decades ago, reacting to today's challenges with yesterday's wiring.

This isn't about blaming your parents, your teachers, or your third-grade spelling bee judge. It's about getting honest with yourself. Ask:

- What beliefs did I form early in life that I still carry today?

- Who or what influenced how I handle failure, risk, or feedback?

- Am I leading today from my *current* self or from a much younger, less equipped version of me?

Take a few minutes here. Reflect on your own childhood. Were you supported or constantly corrected? Did you have space to explore, or were you told to stay within certain lines? Was your home calm and consistent or unpredictable, creating a survival first mindset that now shows up as control, perfectionism, or hesitation?

These aren't easy questions, but they are powerful ones, because the moment you identify where your mindset began, you unlock the ability to change it, and that's what we're here to do.

Social Conditions and Environment

Just as your childhood can influence your mindset, your social conditions and environment also play a significant role. How your parents and caregivers spoke to you, the culture you're used to, and even your school and work environment contribute to creating your mindset. In certain cultures, hard work and persistence are emphasized, reinforcing a **resilient mindset**. However, in other cultures and through certain social norms, natural talent and outer beauty are more heavily valued, which can shape your **mindset**. And yes, how your gender is treated in your culture also plays a major role in whether you learn to push forward or quietly stay in your lane.

Culture plays a big role in shaping who we believe we are. That influence isn't handed out equally. In many parts of the world, boys are raised with a growth-oriented mindset. They're encouraged to take risks, speak up, fail forward, and go after what they want. Girls, on the other hand, are often handed a more rigid mindset. They're taught to play it safe, stay quiet, and prioritize the needs and goals of others over their own.

Now, this isn't about criticizing cultures, it's about naming the patterns that shape us. These are observations, not attacks.

I lived in a culture like that. I wasn't allowed to drive. I wasn't encouraged to think for myself. I was made to believe I would never amount to anything as a woman. I felt helpless, hopeless, and I believed it not because it was true, but because it was told to me so many times it became familiar. Familiar became the truth. That's how a **rigid mindset** takes root: quiet repetition.

Mindset, once again, became the shift that changed everything. The same brain that absorbed those messages had the capacity to question them. To rewire them. I am who I am today because I challenged the beliefs I was handed, and I chose a different path, one thought at a time. Your environment may have influenced your mindset, but it doesn't get the final say. **You do.**

And then there's modern-day environmental influence: social media.

Let's be real, there's nothing like a scroll through curated highlight reels to convince you that your kitchen isn't clean enough, your business isn't big enough, and your life is somehow lagging behind. Influencers, brands, and experts post perfectly lit snapshots of success: smooth skin, thriving careers, stylish homes, and angelic kids who've apparently never thrown a tantrum in public. When that's what your brain consumes daily, it starts doing what brains do best: adapting.

But it doesn't adapt upward. It adapts by lowering your self-worth and increasing self-doubt.

A 2018 study from the University of Pennsylvania found that limiting social media use to just 30 minutes a day significantly reduced anxiety, depression, and feelings of inadequacy. That's not accidental. That's **neuroplasticity** at work. Your brain is always adjusting based on input, and if your daily input is filtered, flawless content that only shows half the story, it's easy to start believing you'll never measure up.

Over time, that constant comparison becomes a mental groove. You start to believe that effort isn't enough, that you don't belong in the room, and that others are simply wired for more. That is the foundation of a **rigid mindset,** and it's not just built by upbringing, but by algorithms.

So take a moment to pause and ask yourself: How has your environment, both online and offline, shaped the way you see yourself? What messages are you absorbing without even realizing it? And are those messages helping or hurting your mindset?

Before you rewire anything, you have to recognize what's been quietly programming you all along.

Personal Experiences and Interpretations: The Stories We Tell Ourselves

While childhood and culture lay the foundation, it's often our personal experiences that reinforce, rewrite, or completely reshape our mindset. But here's the part we often miss: It's not just what happens to us, it's what we *make it mean.* That's the moment our mindset is either built up or broken down.

Two people can go through the same setback—being laid off, passed over, or heartbroken—and walk away with two totally different scripts. One spirals into "I'm not good enough." The other? "This is redirection. I wasn't meant to stay there anyway." The event is the same. The interpretation shapes the trajectory.

Why? Because our brains are not passive storage units, they're "meaning" making machines. And left unchecked, they'll turn even small moments into concrete beliefs. One raised eyebrow during a presentation, one dismissive comment in a meeting, and suddenly you're thirty five, playing small in every boardroom because of something that happened in seventh grade.

It's not always the big, obvious traumas that shape our mindset. Often, it's the quiet cues—the glance, the tone, the pause—and how we carried that forward without ever pausing to question it.

So ask yourself:

- Do I assume people are against me?

- Do I interpret feedback as failure?

- Do I confuse familiarity with truth?

This is where **self-leadership** kicks in. Anyone can experience pain, but leaders are the people who choose to reflect on it. Ask yourself: *What did I learn? What did I decide about myself? And does that belief still belong here, or is it just familiar?*

You can't always control what happens to you. But you can get radically honest about how you *internalize* it. The stories you tell yourself aren't just memories, they're instructions. And mindset? It's built from those instructions, one thought at a time.

Why Does It Matter?

Let's say you've started to notice that you lean more toward a **rigid mindset** than a **resilient** one. You've read through the stories, the research, the examples in this chapter, and while it's all interesting, maybe you're thinking: *Okay, but what does any of this have to do with my job? Or my leadership? What does it matter to my professional life if my mom was critical or my teacher embarrassed me in second grade?*

Well, trust me when I say it matters. It matters a lot.

If you believe you're not good enough, it shows up in the way you lead. You second-guess yourself. You shrink in meetings. You overapologize and overexplain. You avoid giving feedback because you're afraid of being disliked. You say yes when you mean no, not out of generosity, but out of fear that saying no makes you less worthy. You chase perfection to avoid criticism. You cling to control because deep down, you don't trust yourself or others.

And it's exhausting.

That kind of mindset creates leaders who play it safe, micromanage, fear feedback, avoid delegation, and resist visibility. You might hustle hard to prove yourself, but feel hollow when the recognition doesn't land because the deeper belief is still whispering, *you're not enough.* So instead of leading from clarity, you lead from fear. Instead of building trust, you build burnout.

This is why mindset work isn't a "nice to have" for leaders; it's the foundation. Your past experiences, whether dramatic or subtle, shaped how you think. And how you think is the filter through which you lead. If that filter is distorted, no amount of skill, strategy, or spreadsheet wizardry will create the impact you're actually capable of.

So no, this isn't about blaming your childhood. It's about understanding your lens. Because when you know where your mindset came from, you get to decide where it goes next.

And that decision? That's where transformation begins.

Mindset and Happiness

Mindset isn't just about productivity hacks or hitting high-performance goals. It's also deeply connected to something more personal and lasting—your happiness, your family, your business, your team, and the people around you. Whether you realize it or not, how you show up shapes how they experience you. Yes, your spreadsheet game matters, but your mental framework? That's what truly sets the tone for how you lead and how people feel under your leadership.

Your own happiness as a leader is strongly linked to how you think. Psychologist Sonja Lyubomirsky found that up to 40% of your happiness is determined by **intentional activity,** meaning how you reframe situations, regulate emotions, and choose your mental lens (Lyubomirsky. 2008). In other words, mindset trumps circumstance.

So if you're constantly overwhelmed, irritable, or emotionally tapped out, the problem might not be your calendar; it might be your mindset. Because here's the truth: **Happy leaders create happy cultures**. And a resilient mindset is the bridge between the two.

Mindset and Success

Success isn't just about being the most talented person in the room. Let's be honest, how many "talented" people do you know who never actually follow through? You can have all the potential in the world, but if a resilient mindset doesn't show up with it, success won't either.

The truth is, what sets successful people apart isn't just raw ability to master their mindset. A strong mindset is what keeps you going when things get tough, when the excitement fades, and when the obstacles start stacking up like unpaid bills. Talent might get you noticed, but it's your mindset that keeps you in the game.

A resilient mindset also gives you something many high performers quietly lack: the ability to take feedback without emotionally unraveling. Let's face it, no one's thrilled to hear "you could've done better." But if every suggestion feels like an attack on your worth, you're going to stay stuck. People with a resilient mindset take feedback as data, not as a personal indictment. They don't spiral, they adapt. They don't break down when faced with obstacles. They pivot, adjust, recalibrate, and try again.

That's what actually moves the needle. It's not luck, not genius, not timing. Just consistent, focused effort fueled by the belief that growth is always possible. Because at the end of the day, success rarely goes to the smartest person in the room; it goes to the one who refused to quit when things got uncomfortable.

Mindset and Vulnerability

Somewhere along the line, vulnerability got a bad reputation, especially in leadership circles. For decades, we were told that strength meant stoicism: Keep your emotions in check, hold it all together, and never let them see you sweat. But that mindset? It doesn't build trust. It builds walls.

The truth is, leaders who are willing to be vulnerable—who are honest about what they don't know, open about challenges, and real about their learning curves—are far more effective than those who hide behind the illusion of perfection. Vulnerability, when grounded in a **resilient mindset**, isn't weakness. It's leadership strength in its most human form.

As researcher and bestselling author Brené Brown puts it:

"Vulnerability is not winning or losing; it's having the courage to show up and be seen when we have no control over the outcome."

And she's right. It takes a different kind of strength to say, *"I don't have all the answers, but I'm willing to figure it out."* That's not failure. That's emotional maturity, self-awareness, and actual confidence (not the fake kind built on title inflation and rigid control). People don't want perfect leaders. They want real ones. And nothing builds trust faster than authenticity laced with humility.

When you lead from a mindset that embraces vulnerability, you give your team permission to do the same. You allow them to ask questions, offer ideas, admit mistakes, and truly grow. That kind of environment doesn't just feel healthier, it actually performs better, because when people stop wasting energy trying to look perfect, they have more energy to become excellent. Vulnerability with the right mindset isn't a liability. It's a leadership advantage.

Mindset Reflection

Now, as we bring this first chapter in for a landing, I want you to pause for a second and celebrate. You didn't skim. You didn't quit. You made it here, which already means you're one step closer to developing a **resilient mindset** and rewiring your brain for success. That's no small thing.

But let's not stop here.

Growth is a journey, not a checkbox. So, before you jump into the next chapter, take a moment to get honest with yourself. These questions aren't just reflective, they're diagnostic. They'll help you assess the current state of your mindset and where you might still be running old scripts.

Ask yourself:

- When I fail, what's the first thing I tell myself?

- How do I respond to feedback or criticism? Do I grow from it or shut down?

- Who do I blame when things don't go according to plan?

- In what area of my life am I still playing small because of fear or self-doubt?

- What would change if I truly believed I could grow in any area I chose?

Your answers will shape your next steps. You don't need to be perfect to start; you just need to be willing.

Chapter 2

Do You Truly Understand
How Your Mind Works?

Leadership begins with understanding your own mind.

–Sally Allen

One of the first steps in changing your mind is getting to know it. Imagine you're moving into a new house. You're excited to unpack and start the next chapter of your life, but something is wrong. You're not sure what it is, but you know something needs to change. You know that some renovations would be good for the property value, but you're not quite sure where to start. What's the first step? Well, you need to know your house before you can decide what needs to change. If you walk into the house blindfolded, you might not be aware of the terracotta kitchen tiles that don't fit with your aesthetic. Without inspecting every nook and cranny, you might not be aware of the mold in the bathroom. Only by getting to know your house will you know which areas to work on.

It's the same with your mind. After Chapter One, you know mindset matters, but do you know where to begin with your own? Do you have the self-awareness to catch yourself when you're stuck in old thought patterns, or are you just blaming traffic and caffeine shortages?

That's exactly what this chapter is here to unpack.

In my work with business professionals, I've seen a familiar pattern: Many assume their thinking is sharp and evolved, but in reality, they're running on beliefs that haven't had an update since flip phones were cool. And hey, no judgement, I've been there too. The truth is, once you start noticing those old mental habits, you can finally do something about them. It's like realizing you've been driving with the parking brake on... for years.

When I was stuck in an abusive work environment, I found myself repeating the same patterns over and over again, hoping something would change, but nothing ever did. Looking back, I was stuck in a loop. I kept choosing the familiar, not because it was good, but because it was what my brain had learned to expect.

What I didn't understand at the time was this: Every time I repeated those patterns, I was reinforcing a broken mindset. I was unknowingly telling my brain, "This is the way we do things," even though the outcomes were painful and destructive. It wasn't until I stood up to my boss for the first time that something shifted. That moment broke the cycle. For the first time, I challenged the script instead of following it, and that one act of courage created space for a different mindset to take root.

Repetition works both ways. The same mechanism that wires in dysfunction can also be used to rewire strength, self-worth, and clarity. But before we can do that, we have to get brutally honest about which thoughts, behaviors, and beliefs need to go, because you can't change what you won't confront. What's the first step to getting to know our minds? Practicing self-awareness.

Mindset and Self-Awareness

Self-Awareness: The Foundation of Emotional Intelligence

Self-awareness is the cornerstone of emotional intelligence and a critical component of a growth mindset. Daniel Goleman, a leading authority on emotional intelligence, emphasizes that without self-awareness, the ability to manage emotions, empathize, and maintain effective relationships is significantly hindered.

Think of self-awareness as holding up a mirror to your inner world—your thoughts, behaviors, and emotions. It's like watching a movie where you're both the protagonist and the audience, noticing your patterns and understanding how your actions impact the people around you. Without this self-awareness, we operate on autopilot, reacting impulsively rather than responding thoughtfully. It's like navigating your home in the dark; despite knowing the layout, you're bound to stub your toe. Turning on the light (cultivating self-awareness) helps you see clearly, avoid unnecessary pain, and make choices aligned with your values and long-term goals.

Goleman outlines five key components of emotional intelligence: self-awareness, self-regulation, motivation, empathy, and social skills. These competencies enable us to navigate challenges, build resilience, and foster meaningful relationships.

In essence, developing self-awareness isn't just about introspection; it's about laying the groundwork for emotional intelligence, which in turn propels personal growth and resilience.

Social Awareness: The Mirror and the Window

Let's talk about the secret sauce of great leadership: **social awareness**. It's not just about being polite or remembering birthdays (though bonus points if you do). It's your ability to *read the room* and *read the people in it*. That means paying attention to body language, tone shifts, subtle expressions, or the silence that suddenly feels heavy. It's knowing when to speak up, when to pause, and when someone needs a quiet check-in after the meeting ends.

I remember sitting in a meeting once and watching a woman who looked like she was barely holding it together. She said all the right things and nodded at all the right times, but there was a heaviness in her face that no spreadsheet could cover up. Something told me to reach out. So I called her afterward.

Her husband had died the day before.

Let that sink in. *The day before.*

First of all, why was she even in the meeting? That's a separate conversation about boundaries and expectations. But what struck me most was how easy it would've been to miss her pain if I hadn't been paying attention.

That's social awareness. It's part of a broader skill called **external self-awareness**, which is knowing how others experience you and being in tune enough to sense what's happening around you even when nothing's being said out loud.

Susan, a leader I once coached, struggled with this. She saw herself as efficient and clear. Her team saw her as intimidating and critical. The disconnect? She couldn't read the room. Once she learned to observe, listen, and soften her approach, her entire leadership presence shifted for the better.

Social awareness is what helps you lead people, not just projects. It's the quiet superpower behind trust, empathy, and connection. If you want to influence others, you have to start by noticing them.

Mindset and Limiting Beliefs

Have you ever looked at a task and immediately thought, *Nope. Not happening. I'm not cut out for this.* Maybe you've convinced yourself you're not qualified enough, not smart enough, or just not "that kind of person." Congratulations, you've just bumped into a **limiting belief**.

Limiting beliefs are deeply held assumptions about ourselves, others, or the world that quietly steer our behavior and often steer us straight into self-sabotage. They're not facts. They're internal scripts, usually written during our childhood or shaped by painful experiences, that tell us what we *can't* do. Our brains are prediction machines, constantly interpreting new data through the lens of past experiences, so if you were told at eight years old that you "weren't leadership material," guess what your adult brain might still be whispering?

I've seen this time and again in coaching. Leaders who appear confident on the outside but carry an internal narrative that sounds like, *I'm not a real leader. I'm just winging it.* And because beliefs drive behavior, those thoughts start shaping how they show up: hesitant, defensive, or overly rigid.

This is where **self-awareness** becomes your best ally. Self-awareness is the capacity to observe your own thoughts without immediately believing them. It's like putting your inner critic on speakerphone so you can decide whether to agree or hang up.

The beauty is that self-awareness doesn't require you to eliminate every negative thought (that's impossible). But it *does* give you the power to pause and say, "Wait a second. Is that true or just familiar?"

When we become aware of our internal narrative, we create space for change. That's the first step toward replacing limiting beliefs with empowering ones rooted not in the past, but in possibility. And yes, your inner critic may protest. Tell it thanks for the input, but you're leading this meeting now.

The Role of Core Values in Shaping Your Mindset

If mindset is the engine of your behavior, then **core values** are the steering wheel. They guide your decisions, shape your reactions, and subtly influence how you show up in every area of life, from your career to your conversations. Core values aren't just lofty ideals you frame on the office wall; they're deeply held beliefs that operate like an internal compass, constantly pointing you toward what matters most. They are, quite literally, your personal truth. Strip away the ego, expectations, people pleasing, and performance, and what remains are your values. Honesty. Growth. Freedom. Connection. Integrity. (Coffee might feel like one, but let's not confuse values with survival tools.)

When you're aware of your core values, decision-making gets clearer. You feel more grounded. You start saying "yes" to the right things and "no" without guilt. But when you're *not* in touch with your values? You make choices that look good on paper but feel wrong in your gut. You overcommit, overexplain, and miss out on the life that's right in front of you.

And here's where things get messy: Most people don't intentionally ignore their values; they're just unaware of them. I've coached leaders who consistently chose safety over growth, even though they claimed to value innovation and bold thinking. The disconnect wasn't in their ambition; it was in their alignment.

This is what psychologists call **cognitive dissonance**—that uncomfortable inner tension that shows up when your actions and values don't match (Festinger, 1957). Over time, that dissonance leads to burnout, stress, and the sinking feeling that you're living someone else's version of success.

The good news is that once you name your values, you can start honoring them. When you're clear on what matters most, your mindset becomes more resilient. You bounce back faster because your choices are rooted in something solid. You lead with integrity, even when it's hard. You trust yourself more because you're no longer outsourcing your identity to the approval of others.

So, if life feels misaligned right now, don't panic. Start here: What values have you been ignoring? What would change if you lived them out loud?

And yes, this may require change, discomfort, even courage, but that's not a sign you're off track; it's a sign you're heading somewhere worth going.

Building Your Core Values: A Step-by-Step Process

Now that we've explored how core values shape your mindset, let's get practical, because knowing values *matter* isn't the same as knowing *yours*. Many people are living by borrowed values passed down from parents, absorbed from culture, or inherited from the workplace, and while some may fit, others act like emotional shapewear: tight, exhausting, and not made for you.

So let's change that.

Here's a powerful, four-step process to help you identify the values that actually align with who you are and who you're becoming.

Step 1: Review the Words

Start with the curated list of value words (you'll find them below, broken up into three sections). Circle every word that resonates from each section. Don't filter, just feel. Do NOT overthink.

Step 2: Narrow Each Section Down to 3-5 Words

The next step is to narrow down each section of your list. Look at the words you circled. Which feel the *most true* to you? Not the ones that sound good. Not the ones you wish you embodied. The ones that actually guide how you live, lead, and decide on your best days and hardest ones. Now pick between three and five of them to keep.

Step 3: Trim to 5

Now comes the refining. From all the words you've selected, which five could act as your North Star? These should reflect what grounds you, fuels you, and guides how you show up in the world. If everything else faded away, these five would still stand. They are your internal compass.

Step 4: Choose Your Core 3

These final three are your *bedrock values*. Define them in your own words. "Freedom" might mean flexibility in your schedule. "Excellence" might mean pushing beyond what's expected. Make them personal. Make them yours. Because when your mindset is built on values you choose, not the ones you inherited, you stop chasing someone else's version of success and start building a life that actually fits.

Core Value Words to Choose From

If you do not see your word here, just add it!

Personal Values

Accountability	Authenticity	Balance	Calm	Clarity
Discipline	Excellence	Faith	Flexibility	Forgiveness
Gratitude	Growth	Harmony	Honesty	Hope
Humility	Integrity	Joy	Mindfulness	Modesty
Openness	Optimism	Patience	Peace	Perseverance
Presence	Purpose	Resilience	Security	Self-discipline
Simplicity	Spirituality	Stability	Success	Trust
Wisdom	Zeal			

Relational Values

Belonging	Care	Collaboration	Communication	Compassion
Connection	Empathy	Equality	Fairness	Family
Friendship	Generosity	Honoring others	Inclusivity	Kindness
Listening	Love	Loyalty	Nurturing	Open-mindedness
Respect	Responsibility	Service	Support	

Leadership Values

Ambition	Appreciation	Assertiveness	Awareness	Bravery
Commitment	Community	Competence	Confidence	Consciousness
Contribution	Cooperation	Courage	Creativity	Curiosity
Determination	Dignity	Empowerment	Enthusiasm	Faithfulness
Fortitude	Impact	Independence	Influence	Ingenuity
Innovation	Insight	Justice	Leadership	Learning
Meaning	Passion	Reliability	Resourcefulness	Self-expression
Vision				

Building Habits That Align With Core Values

Using Your Core Values to Make Confident, Mindful Decisions

Once you've identified your core values, the next step is learning how to *use* them, especially when making decisions that carry emotional or strategic weight. This is where mindset and values intersect. Pro-tip: Now use those value words to create a one line mission statement for your life.

Your **mindset** is the lens through which you interpret the world—your beliefs, your patterns, your inner narrative. Your **values** are the framework that gives that lens focus. Together, they help you move through uncertainty with clarity and conviction.

Life isn't short on options. What it lacks, especially in high-pressure leadership and growth seasons, is alignment. When your mindset is rooted in your core values, you stop spinning in self-doubt and start making grounded, confident decisions.

Here's how I apply it. My core values are **faith, courage, family, impact, and value**. Every major decision I make runs through those five filters. Let's use writing this book as an example.

- **Faith:** Writing this book requires me to move forward without guarantees. Some days, I wonder if it will make an impact. I question my voice. I doubt whether I'm the one to write it. But faith means trusting the process before the proof shows up. It means acting in alignment with who I'm becoming, not just what I see in front of me. Faith isn't about certainty; it's about commitment, even when the outcome is unclear.

- **Courage:** Am I willing to put my voice out there, knowing I might face critique or doubt? Yes. And let's be real, growth never comes from hiding.

- **Family:** Will this take from the people who matter most? No. I've structured my schedule so I can create without compromising connection.

- **Impact:** Will this serve others in a meaningful way? Yes. And that belief keeps my mindset focused on purpose, not perfection.

- **Value:** Will it offer real, lasting transformation? Yes. If it didn't, I wouldn't write it.

That's five for five. That's alignment.

This framework allows me to move forward without any second-guessing or guilt. And if the answer to one of those value check questions had been "no," that wouldn't be failure, it would be feedback. A prompt to recalibrate, not abandon.

Your values aren't just ideals. They are your internal board of directors. Invite them to the table every time a big decision shows up. And if all five nod in agreement? You've got your answer, no spreadsheet or presentation required.

Mindset Reflection

The next time you're stuck in indecision or flooded with options, pause and ask yourself:

- Is this choice aligned with my values?

- Does it support the mindset I want to live in, not just today, but long-term?

- Am I moving from fear or from faith?

- Would future me be proud of this decision?

- If I didn't need approval or certainty, what would I choose right now?

When the answers point to alignment, you can move forward with peace, clarity, and power.

Chapter 3

Leading Your Thoughts—Because Your Greatest Challenge Is You

The quality of your leadership will never exceed the quality of your thinking.

–Sally Allen

In the previous chapter, we talked about mindset and core values acting as your internal compass. Now, let's zoom in further on the actual driver of that compass: your thoughts.

Here's the truth no leadership book wants to put on the cover: **Your greatest leadership challenge won't be your team.** It will be leading yourself. Specifically, leading your thoughts, because if you don't learn to guide them, they will absolutely take the wheel, and let's just say, your brain unsupervised is not always the best driver.

I had the incredible opportunity to speak with Captain Michelle Tavarez of the Las Vegas Metro Police Department on my podcast, and I asked her about self-leadership. She said it all starts in the mind. One strategy she teaches is called *Crisis Rehearsal*—training yourself to mentally walk through difficult scenarios while visualizing a successful outcome. As Michelle puts it, "Your body cannot go where your mind has never been." In moments of uncertainty, whether on duty or when making leadership decisions, she practices proactive mindset work. You do not manifest failure. You visualize success, all the way to the end. Your thoughts shape your mindset, your mindset shapes your leadership, and good leadership, like it or not, is contagious.

I've seen it firsthand. A leader walks into a room with a rigid, negative mindset filled with fear, resistance, or frustration, and soon the entire team mirrors it. Deadlines slip, innovation stalls, and culture starts to crack, not because the team lacked skill, but because the leader's mindset became the ceiling.

So, how do you fix that?

You start by leading you. That means building awareness of the stories you tell yourself. It means challenging assumptions, reframing failure, and choosing curiosity over criticism. It's not about pretending everything is great; it's about refusing to let your thoughts run wild and take the rest of the company down with them.

So consider this your daily job description: Lead your mind first. Then lead your people. In that order. Because the quality of your leadership will never exceed the quality of your thinking.

Here's a link to the podcast episode with Captain Michelle Tavarez:

How Do I Start Leading My Thoughts?

At this point, you might be wondering, *How do I actually start leading my thoughts, Sally?* It starts with self-awareness. Quiet, consistent, sometimes inconvenient, but deeply powerful awareness.

Before we jump in, I want to share with you something from my interview with Greg Anderson, CEO and President of Allegiant Air. He shared that self-awareness is foundational to leadership. Great leadership starts with knowing yourself. Greg spoke about the importance of self-improvement and emotional intelligence, and how critical it becomes as your level of responsibility rises. The higher the responsibility, the deeper the inner work.

Self-awareness isn't just about noticing your moods. It's about recognizing the ripple effect of your internal state on the people around you. Are you showing up with clarity or chaos? Confidence or control? Greg emphasized that when a leader lacks self-awareness, their team is the first to feel it, even if no one says it out loud. You can't manage others if you're constantly being managed by your own unexamined emotions.

When your mind begins spinning, whether from pressure, fear, or just the sheer noise of the day, pause and ask yourself a few grounding questions. *What thoughts have I been entertaining today? Are they rooted in truth, or just fear wearing a very convincing costume? Would I actually follow someone who's thinking the way I'm thinking right now?* It's a humbling check-in, but a necessary one. But remember, if the answer is no, that's not a personal failure. It's a signal. A flashing neon invitation to shift.

One of the most powerful tools you can use to reset your mindset in that moment is your core values. Being self-aware also means knowing which values drive you and using them as anchors when your thoughts try to drift. When things feel chaotic or reactive, ask yourself: *Which of my values can I lean on right now?* Maybe it's courage. Maybe it's grace. Maybe it's discipline. Let that value recalibrate your thinking and remind you of who you are beneath the noise.

And then ask yourself: *What shift in mindset would best serve both me and the people I lead right now?* That's not a trick question. It's a leadership moment. One that great leaders don't outsource. They practice the pause. They assess, they reframe, and they respond with intentionality, not impulse because leading well isn't just behavior; it's belief in motion. And belief begins in thought.

Here's a link to the podcast episode with Greg Anderson:

Mastering The Leader's Mindset

Your Mindset Sets the Tone For Everyone

To summarize what we have covered so far: Your mindset isn't just a personal trait; it's a leadership tool, a cultural thermostat, and a mirror your team is constantly reading. It quietly (or not so quietly) shapes how you lead, how others respond to you, and ultimately, how far your team and organization can grow. Simply put, the way you think influences the way you lead and the way your people live and work under your leadership.

We've established that mindset is the lens through which you interpret challenges, relationships, and opportunities, but here's where it gets real: If that lens is fogged up by fear, rigidity, ego, or self-doubt, it will distort everything. You'll miss possibilities, you'll misread people, and you'll likely mismanage situations that require vision, empathy, or nuance.

The Importance of Resilience and Adaptability

We live in a fast-changing world. The kind where today's best practices are outdated by next quarter, and stability is mostly a nice thought. That means resilience and adaptability are not bonus traits for leaders. They are survival skills. Every organization wants someone who can stay steady in the storm and flexible in the shift because that builds trust, momentum, and keeps the team from spiraling every time a curveball hits. A resilient leader does not crumble under pressure. They recover from setbacks, adapt in real time, and keep moving forward without losing their clarity or calling HR from the break room floor.

Let's be honest. Life throws curveballs. Business throws entire plot twists. It is not a question of if challenges will come, but simply a matter of when. The best way to prepare is not by tightening control, but by building a mindset that can bend without breaking.

Resilience is not about pretending failure does not hurt. It is about refusing to be defined by it. The most grounded leaders learn from the fall instead of letting it flatten them. Think about a moment in your life when you were knocked down but got back up. Maybe not right away. Maybe not without a few tears or snacks involved. But you freaking did it. That story counts. It does not need to be a polished business example. Some of your strongest mindset muscles come from your personal life, not boardroom wins.

Those personal moments shape your professional mindset. The messy ones. The rebuilds. The times you started from scratch with nothing but a prayer and a to-do list. When you lead from that place, people trust you because they know you have been through something and did not let it take you out.

Now let's talk about adaptability. While resilience keeps you grounded, adaptability keeps you relevant. It is your ability to pivot when plans fall apart, adjust when systems shift, and evolve when the universe clearly did not get your calendar. And here is the thing: Your team is watching how you respond to change. If you resist it, they will fear it. If you panic, they will pull back. But if you meet it with curiosity, creativity, and a deep breath that does not involve screaming into a pillow, you give them permission to stay engaged.

That does not mean you will always enjoy change. You are human after all. Sometimes change is terrifying, but instead of avoiding it, ask yourself what you are really afraid of. What is the worst that could happen? Then ask what might actually go right. Lay both out on the table. Then choose which one you are going to lead from because whatever you model, your team will reflect.

Adaptability does not mean you love the chaos. It means you know how to move through it. And when your people see you doing that with clarity, calm, and a little grit, they will rise too. Not because it is easy, but because you showed them how.

How Mindset Impacts Emotional Intelligence

We live in a world that loves to celebrate high IQ. We admire the Sherlock-types who can solve a crisis with nothing but a pencil and sheer brainpower. And hey, being smart is great. But somewhere in our obsession with genius, we've overlooked another kind of intelligence—the kind that keeps people from rage-quitting in meetings or crying in the break room. Emotional intelligence (EQ).

EQ is often more important than IQ, especially for leaders. It's your ability to recognize, understand, and manage your own emotions while also navigating the emotional waves of others. Basically, it's knowing when to speak, when to listen, and when to close your laptop before you say something you'll regret.

Effective leadership demands EQ, and at the root of strong emotional intelligence is one thing most people don't think about: your mindset. This is because your mindset shapes how you interpret emotions. A fixed mindset might treat emotions like a nuisance—something to suppress or avoid—but a growth mindset knows emotions are signals. They tell you what's working, what's not, and how your team really feels about the way you lead. Spoiler: It's not always what you think.

Emotional intelligence isn't just about keeping your cool. It's about reading the room, adjusting your approach, and responding in ways that build trust. Combine a positive mindset with strong EQ, and you get leadership that people actually want to follow. The kind that doesn't just manage outcomes, but manages energy, relationships, and resilience.

IQ might win trivia night, but EQ builds teams that don't implode under pressure.

Leading By Example

Your mindset might feel like a personal thing...like something you keep tucked away behind your morning coffee and polite smiles—but that's not quite how it works. As a leader, your mindset is on full display, whether you realize it or not. It shows up in how you respond under pressure, how you treat others, and how you handle failure when no one claps for your effort. Over time, your mindset quietly becomes the blueprint for your team's culture.

If you face challenges with curiosity and calm, your team learns to do the same, but if you react with fear and rigidity, guess what? They'll start bracing for impact anytime things get hard. Your mindset doesn't stay in your head. It ripples. It echoes. It spreads. And depending on what state your mindset is in, that can be really good news or a leadership horror story waiting to happen.

If you're carrying a negative mindset, you might be unintentionally leading your team into a low-trust, poor-communication, burnout culture where silence feels safer than feedback. But if you're leading with a growth-oriented, grounded mindset, you're building something better—more collaboration, higher morale, and a team that bounces back instead of burning out.

The way you think becomes the way your team feels, and how they feel drives how they perform.

Now I get it. That might be a little uncomfortable to hear, especially if you know you're not yet the leader you want to be. If you're feeling overwhelmed or even slightly guilty for leading from a rigid mindset, pause and take a breath. There's no shame, no panic, and no resignation letter needed. Breathe out the guilt and breathe in the truth that you can shift this, because you can.

Section One may have pointed out some hard truths, but don't worry. Section Two is where we start to work on the solution. Before we dive in, though, I've got one practical step you can take right now, because real change starts with awareness, and you're already ahead just by being willing to look.

Mindset Reflection

Imagine you're leading a team on an important project. Despite weeks of planning, the deadline was missed due to a combination of unexpected challenges and communication breakdowns. The client is frustrated, and tensions are high within the team. Now, I want you to imagine two possible outcomes to this scenario: one where the leader has a rigid mindset and one where the leader has a resilient mindset. How do you think the scenario would play out in these two teams? Which one would you like to be? What can you learn by watching these two scenarios play out before you?

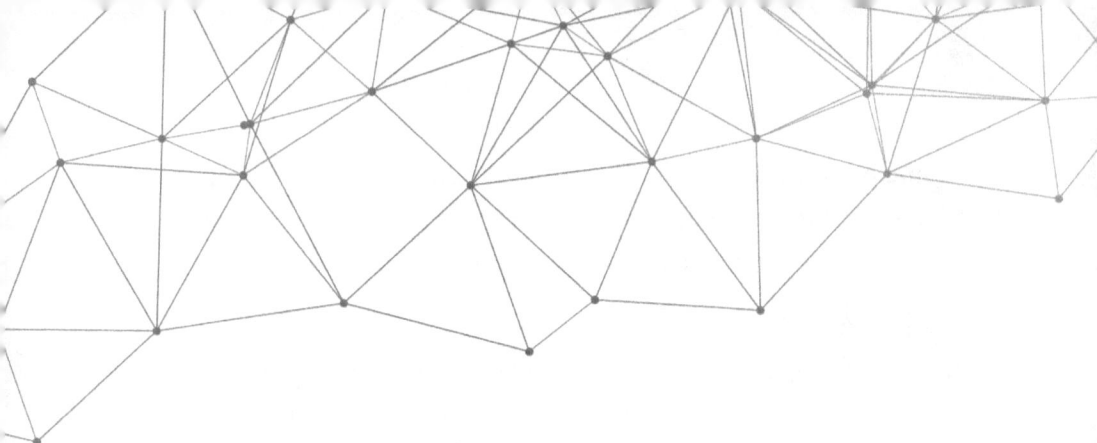

Section 2: The Solution

Mastering your mindset isn't about avoiding challenges, it's about knowing how to navigate them with clarity and confidence.

–Sally Allen

With the science under our belt, we've built a solid foundation for what's coming next: the solution. A solution for what, you might ask? For that nagging feeling of being stuck. For the hamster wheel you've been sprinting on with Olympic-level effort but zero forward motion. It's the solution to shifting your mindset in a way that actually lasts. And yes, I know that probably sounds like something off a podcast ad for brain gummies, but stay with me.

I've met more than my fair share of skeptics over the years. People who've read every buzzword-packed, AI-generated, quick-fix mindset book out there. And I get it. The market is flooded with noise. But this is different. This framework actually works. I've seen it in real time, over and over again, with the leaders, professionals, and teams I've coached. No magic. No fluff. Just practical steps with real results.

Is it some complex reinvention of human psychology that requires charts, a PhD, and a vision board? Nope, not even close. One of the reasons this method works so well is that it's simple, and because it's simple, it sticks.

This solution is called The MINDSET Framework. It's seven steps to rewire your thinking and shift from a fixed mindset to a growth one. Each step is represented by a letter in the word mindset, so you can remember it without needing to tattoo it on your arm. What makes it powerful is the combination of reflection and action. It's not just theory you'll nod along to; it's built for real-life application as you move through this book.

If you're a curious cat like I am, here's your sneak peek at what each step of The MINDSET Framework includes.

- M: Move to Pause

- I: Identify the Trigger

- N: Name the Thought

- D: Dissect the Belief

- S: Shift Your Perspective

- E: Engage in Action

- T: Track Your Progress

Over the course of this section, we'll walk through each letter of the MINDSET Framework one chapter at a time. Each step is its own milestone, and each milestone matters. This isn't a checklist. It's a process of transformation, and like all meaningful growth, it's not meant to be rushed.

If some of these steps feel familiar, good! That means the science section worked. You're already primed to take action. If some steps feel foreign, that's good too. That means your brain is paying attention and stretching.

What's most important is that you resist the urge to skip ahead. That temptation will come, especially if you're an overachiever or someone who secretly likes to "peek at the last chapter," but rewiring your mind isn't a speed read kind of journey. Your brain will need time to unlearn, reframe, and rebuild.

So don't be surprised when your mind resists. That's biology. Your brain has been working hard to keep you in familiar patterns, even the ones that hold you back. It sees your current mindset as "safe," even if it's sabotaging your goals. So, when you start redirecting your thoughts and building a new mindset, you can expect some pushback.

Be kind to yourself, but also be resilient. You're not here for surface change. You're here for real change.

When I started my own business, I was terrified. I'd spent years in more traditional roles, where security came with a salary and a structure. Suddenly, it was just me, a vision, and a whole lot of self-doubt. My mindset screamed, *Who do you think you are?* But deep down, I knew the answer: I was someone who had to try. So I did. I took the leap and built new mental muscles along the way. That choice to lead my mind instead of letting fear lead me was one of the most pivotal moments I've ever made.

Changing your mindset isn't comfortable. But it *is* transformational.

Chapter 4

M—Move to Pause

The strongest leaders aren't the ones without fear,
they're the ones who don't let fear decide for them.

–Sally Allen

Imagine for a moment you're at your desk, living out one of *those* days.

You're behind schedule, two team members are mid-conflict in the hallway like it's a reality show, and your inbox has declared a silent mutiny. On top of it all, you were passed over again for that promotion you were quietly hoping for. The day isn't just stressful; it's personal.

And amidst the noise, a familiar thought pushes its way to the front of your mind: *"I'm not good enough. This is as far as I'll go. I should probably just give up."*

We've all been there. That mental spiral where one hard moment becomes a sweeping declaration about your worth, your future, and your career. Here's the catch, though: When the pressure is on, your brain doesn't typically get more accurate. In fact, it usually gets more dramatic. You default to old patterns, half-truths, and worst-case narratives not because you're broken, but because you're human.

This is where our framework begins. The first step to shifting your mindset is to **Move to Pause**.

Why "move" to pause? Because let's be honest: Pausing doesn't come naturally in chaos. Our instinct is usually to react, overfunction, fix, or retreat. Pausing isn't passive; it's a deliberate move. A *choice* to step out of the emotional current and notice what's actually going on in your thoughts. Think of it as hitting the brakes, not because you're quitting, but because you're taking control of the wheel.

Moving to pause gives you the space to interrupt the default script. It's the moment where you stop letting your thoughts run you and start leading them. That one, small decision creates the mental margin needed to shift everything that follows.

Now, let's be clear. This isn't the same as "fake it till you make it." Rewiring your mindset isn't about pretending everything's fine. It's about lifting the mental rug and figuring out where the funky smell is really coming from. It's honest, it's intentional and it's the opposite of avoidance.

When I first started coaching, I didn't even want to stop and think about it. Me? Coaching? Who was I to help anyone? I was afraid that if I slowed down long enough to really consider it, I'd talk myself right out of it.

I didn't want to pause. I wanted to power through. I was scared, under-resourced, and convinced everyone else had it figured out. But trying to outrun my thoughts didn't make them go away. It wasn't until I gave myself permission to slow down that things began to shift. I had to learn how to pause, reflect, and recognize what I actually had to offer the world so that I could then embrace it.

So, if you're stuck, discouraged, or drowning in overthinking, don't press harder.

Press pause. On purpose. With authority. Like a leader.

THE POWER OF PAUSING

I don't know if you remember, but back in 2016, there was a viral trend called the **Mannequin Challenge**. The idea? People would freeze in place like mannequins while someone recorded a video moving through the scene. Whole classrooms, offices, weddings, and even NBA teams participated, holding dramatic or hilarious poses while Rae Sremmurd's "Black Beatles" played in the background. The fun of it was in the stillness. For a few seconds, time stopped.

Now, was it a little silly? Sure. But it reminds us of something powerful: **Sometimes we need to pause to see clearly.**

The first step of rewiring your mindset is your own internal mannequin moment. Not because you're going to freeze and avoid the chaos, but because you're going to interrupt it. The pause isn't passivity; it's power.

Let me tell you about Luke, one of my executive clients who, when we met, didn't know how to stop moving. I don't mean physically (although his calendar looked like a game of Tetris). I mean mentally. Luke was in constant solve it, fix it, prove it mode. His team called him "the fireman" because he jumped into every crisis, every decision, every little detail. Usually with good intentions, but often without clarity.

He didn't pause to assess the situation or listen to both sides. He just charged in, assuming speed would equal effectiveness. When something went wrong, Luke responded instantly. He would fire off a corrective email, jump into meetings midstream, and start solving problems before he even understood what the actual issue was. It wasn't malicious. It was just his default setting. Move faster, do more, fix it now!

But what Luke didn't realize was that his speed was creating confusion. His team wasn't learning, they were waiting. Waiting for him to jump in. Waiting for the answer. Waiting to be rescued. His leadership wasn't empowering; it was reactive, and while he thought he was helping, he was actually training his team to depend on him for everything.

Eventually, he burned out. Hard.

When we started coaching, the hardest thing for him wasn't making decisions. It was doing *nothing* even for five seconds. We practiced the pause. Not dramatic meditation breaks or days off the grid (though those are great, too). Just simple moments of intentional stillness before responding. We called it his "mental comma."

Over time, Luke began to notice something. In the space of the pause, he gained clarity. He responded more thoughtfully, his team began stepping up, and, ironically, the less he rushed, the more respected and effective he became.

This is the invitation for you, too.

In a world that trains us to equate velocity with value, pausing can feel like falling behind, but it's not. **It's a mindset move. A leadership muscle. A necessary reset.** Because if your brain is in overdrive, your leadership won't run on strategy, it'll run on stress.

So no, you don't have to freeze in place like a mannequin while someone films you, but you do need to interrupt the noise. Give yourself space to observe your thoughts before you let them shape your actions.

Move to Pause. Not to stop, but to regain control. That's where transformation begins.

What Does It Mean to Pause?

Pausing means creating a conscious moment of space between what's happening and how you respond. It means catching your breath before walking into a meeting with two coworkers who are one email away from a workplace cage match. It means unclenching your jaw before responding to that delightful client who thinks your job is to absorb their emotional chaos. Pausing is what allows you to shift from reacting on autopilot to choosing your response with intention, and here's the best part—you don't even have to fix the response yet. All you need to do in this step is breathe. One breath. In. Out. Simple, right? Which is exactly why most people skip it.

When you pause, you give your brain a chance to register what's actually happening, both internally and externally. You get to notice what emotion is rising without letting it hijack your next move. That pause becomes the opening where you can step back from the swirl of overthinking, self-doubt, or impulse, and realign with who you actually want to be in that moment. In leadership, this isn't just helpful; it's essential. That split-second pause can be the difference between escalating conflict or resolving it. Between delivering criticism or offering coaching. Between pushing through to burnout or choosing to lead from balance.

The Science Behind Pausing

By now, you might be thinking, "Alright, I get it! The pause is important. But what's actually happening in my brain when I do that?" Great question. Because this isn't just feel good advice. It's rooted in science.

Let's talk a bit more about your amygdala.

This almond shaped part of your brain is responsible for scanning for danger. It's what triggers your **fight, flight, or freeze** response when something feels threatening, whether that something is a snarling dog, a near miss on the freeway, or your VP's tone in a meeting. The amygdala's job is to protect you, and when real danger is present, it's a superhero. You want that instinct to kick in when something's flying at your face.

Here's the problem: Under chronic stress or emotional pressure, your amygdala doesn't know the difference between a bear in the woods and a bad Slack message. This is what Dr. Daniel Goleman, author of *Emotional*

Intelligence, coined as the "**amygdala hijack**" (1995). When it takes over, your thinking brain gets temporarily overridden. You stop reflecting and start reacting, and while that might keep you alive in the wilderness, it does you zero favors in a boardroom or team conflict.

This is why a stressed-out leader tends to become rigid, defensive, or impulsive. The amygdala floods your system with urgency, making small issues feel like code red emergencies. Suddenly, your tone sharpens, your perspective narrows, and you're making snap decisions or worse, no decisions at all.

So what happens when you **pause**?

You activate your prefrontal cortex, the executive center of the brain responsible for rational thinking, problem solving, empathy, and long-term strategy. This is where your resilient mindset lives. It's the part of your brain that allows you to zoom out, consider context, and lead with clarity rather than emotion.

Even a *brief* pause is enough to interrupt the amygdala hijack. When you take a breath, the prefrontal cortex signals the amygdala to stand down. The intensity lowers. Emotional reactivity softens. Suddenly, you're not just reacting, you're thinking, leading, and choosing.

Let that sink in: **A single pause can shift you from survival mode to strategic mode.**

The science is clear: Your best thinking doesn't come from the part of your brain that's panicking. It comes from the part that knows how to slow down, get perspective, and lead forward.

So the next time your stress flares and your thoughts start racing, remember this: You're wise for letting your brain catch up to your leadership.

Responding vs. Reacting

As a result of pausing, you gain something powerful: the ability to respond instead of react. Now, those two words might sound similar, but don't let that fool you. The difference between them often defines the kind of leader you become. Are you the one who lashes out in the heat of the moment, or the one who addresses conflict with clarity and calm? Because only one of those earns long-term respect. And spoiler alert—it's not the one who storms out of the Zoom room.

Reacting is fast, instinctive, and emotional. It's your brain's way of protecting you by going straight to survival mode. Unfortunately, survival mode has a terrible track record in performance reviews, tough conversations, and team meetings where the stakes feel high. Reacting pulls from fear, frustration, and unresolved baggage. It's a reflex, and while it has its place, like if you're running from a bear or stepping on a Lego, it's not the mindset you want guiding your leadership.

Responding, on the other hand, is slower. It's intentional. It comes from awareness and alignment with your values. It says, "I see what's happening, and I'm choosing how to handle it." That one second of space between the trigger and the reaction? That's where leadership lives.

In short, reacting is automatic. Responding is a decision.

As a leader, choosing response over reaction changes everything. Yes, reacting has its moments of glory, like swerving to avoid a rogue shopping cart, but everyday leadership is not a crisis zone. Even though, let's be honest, some office politics might *feel* like psychological warfare, your life is probably not in actual danger. So no, you don't need to go full fight-or-flight when someone challenges your decision in a meeting. You just need to pause.

That pause gives your higher self a chance to step in—the one that's grounded in purpose, not ego. The self that leads from wisdom, not wounds. When you don't pause, you're more likely to react from fear, insecurity, or the old belief that you need to prove something. Those fear-based responses are rooted in stories that no longer serve you. Stories that tell you you're not enough. That you have to defend your worth at all costs. But that thinking will lock you into a rigid mindset and keep you in emotional survival mode.

The pause is the bridge between fear and freedom. It's the space where you reclaim your leadership and choose to respond from power, not panic. That choice is where everything starts to shift.

When to Pause?

One of the most overlooked leadership skills is knowing when to sit your brilliant self down and pause. Not as a nice-to-have. As a non-negotiable.

Let's be honest. Most leaders aren't lacking action. They're lacking awareness. They charge into decisions, drag stress into meetings like it's a plus-one, and treat adrenaline like a strategy. But your ability to pause is directly linked to your ability to lead with clarity instead of chaos.

Here's when you need to hit pause:

- **You're emotionally hijacked.** Your jaw is tight, your face is hot, and you're two seconds away from replying to that email with "Per my last freaking message." When cortisol spikes, cognition drops. Pausing is psychological first aid.

- **You're reacting to everything but solving nothing.** Your day feels like whack-a-mole. You're busy but not productive. That scattered feeling is your nervous system screaming for help. Even a 90-second pause can reset your mental bandwidth and help you shift back into strategy mode.

- **You don't care anymore.** You're nodding in meetings, but inside you feel numb or disconnected. This isn't laziness. It's depletion or misalignment. Pausing helps you reconnect to your purpose before burnout starts making decisions for you.

- **You're mentally foggy.** You don't know what to say or which direction to take. Your brain is buffering. That's not failure. It's a cue to stop forcing clarity and give your mind space to sort things out.

- **You're addicted to urgency.** Everything feels like a fire drill. You've mistaken hustle for leadership. Pausing lets you zoom out, reassess priorities, and stop treating every task like it's life or death.

The best leaders don't just act. They align. They pause with purpose because clarity, courage, and credibility don't live in chaos. They live in the pause.

How To Pause

Knowing you need to pause is a powerful start, but real growth comes from knowing how to do it with intention. This framework is designed to move beyond theory and into practice. You've already learned why pausing matters. Now it's time to explore how to integrate it into your daily leadership. Pausing in the middle of stress or overwhelm may not come naturally at first, but it can be trained. Like any leadership skill, it becomes easier with repetition, especially when you have a structure to follow. Over the years, I've helped countless leaders build this exact skill, and I've found that one method in particular creates consistent, lasting results.

To help you build the discipline of pausing in real time without losing your momentum, I recommend you follow the five-step process outlined in the next section. Each step is simple, powerful, and designed to ground you in clarity and intention, even in high-pressure moments. Let's walk through each one together.

Step 1: Stop Physically

The first move in any real mindset shift? You have to **interrupt the moment**.

That means physically stopping what you're doing. Close the laptop. Unclench your jaw. Lower your voice. Take your fingers off the keyboard like they're about to send an email you'll regret. Whatever action is tied to your reactive thought loop, pause it.

This isn't just behavioral. It's **biological**. That small physical interruption sends a signal to your nervous system: *We're not in danger, we're in leadership.* When you stop the motion, you disrupt the momentum of stress. It's your way of saying, *We're not going to let this moment own us.*

I've seen senior leaders shift entire meeting dynamics with one simple gesture: pushing back from the table, leaning in with intention, or going quiet for a full breath. Those moves don't weaken their authority. They **amplify** it. Because presence under pressure is power.

This type of interruption trains your brain to engage a new pathway, one that favors choice over chaos. And here's the secret: The more you practice, the faster it works. With time, you'll notice the warning signs sooner and catch yourself before you spiral.

So no, it's not dramatic. It's deliberate. It's leadership in action.

Step 2: Change Your Environment

Once you've interrupted the moment, the next move is simple but strategic: **change your environment**.

Get up. Step away from the screen. Walk toward a window, down the hallway, or over to the kitchen. You're not fleeing, you're creating space. Any movement away from the physical center of tension helps tell your brain: *We're shifting out of reactivity and into reflection.* This physical relocation matters because it breaks the rhythm of stress and signals your nervous system that the threat has passed. It gives your body a chance to reset, and your mind the room to reorient.

One executive I coached started doing this religiously. After years of reacting too quickly in meetings, she made it a practice to physically leave the room, even just for a minute, when conversations got tense. Her leadership presence changed almost overnight. Instead of being seen as reactive, she became known for her calm, measured insight.

It wasn't a personality shift. It was a strategy shift.

Changing your environment gives you a chance to take control of your presence before re-engaging. It doesn't take long, but it makes a lasting difference.

So, next time the pressure starts building, don't stay frozen in the chaos. Take a walk, get some air, and reclaim your clarity.

This is where your leadership posture begins to shift.

Step 3: Regulate Through Breath

Once you've paused and stepped into a different space, it's time to reconnect with something simple but powerful: **your breath.**

Intentional breathing is one of the fastest, most effective ways to bring your nervous system back into balance. And the best part? You always have access to it, no login required.

When you take a slow, deliberate inhale through your nose and exhale gently through your mouth, you activate your **parasympathetic nervous system**. This is the part of your body responsible for calming things down, lowering cortisol, and signaling to your brain: *We're safe now. You can lead.*

This isn't deep breathing in a "spa music and herbal tea" kind of way. It's neuroscience-backed self-regulation. Studies from Stanford's Center for Mindfulness show that even **one intentional breath** can shift your brain out of fight-or-flight and into a state where logic, empathy, and executive function return online.

You don't need five minutes in the lotus position. Just one or two conscious breaths is all it takes to recenter and reclaim your internal authority.

If you prefer structure, try **box breathing,** a method used by Navy SEALs to stay calm under pressure (Balban, et al., 2023). It's simple:

- Inhale for 4 seconds.

- Hold for 4 seconds.

- Exhale for 4 seconds.

- Hold empty for 4 seconds.

- Repeat for 4–5 cycles.

Breathing doesn't mean you're checking out, it means you're checking in. And in high-stakes leadership, that's exactly what strengthens your presence.

Step 4: Remind Yourself of Your Values and Control

In the space you've created mentally, you can now check in with your core values. Ask yourself questions like:

- Who do I want to be right now?
- What matters most in this moment?
- What outcome aligns with my bigger vision?

In doing so, you will also reclaim your sense of agency. You get to remind yourself that you have control over how you choose to respond. Your response isn't at the mercy of the moment.

These four steps might seem overly simple, but don't overlook their effectiveness. With something as simple as these short steps, you can interrupt the negative cycle swimming in your head, allowing you to think clearly and grow as a leader.

Mindset Reflection

Before we move on to step two, let's take some time to really think about what we've learned in this chapter. Take a moment to consider the following questions and give yourself enough time to really sink into each one.

- Think of a time in your career when you felt overwhelmed and reacted poorly. Do you think pausing would've helped in that moment? How?

- What's the biggest reason why you don't pause more often? How can you change that?

- What method would you like to try first to help with pausing, and why?

- What can you do to remind yourself to pause and use the method you just identified?

- How would your team benefit if you move to pause more often?

Chapter 5

I—Identify the Trigger

A leader's true power is in recognizing what triggers
them and choosing to respond rather than react.

–Sally Allen

The Truth About Triggers

Emotions are often treated like mythical creatures: hard to track, poorly understood, and occasionally terrifying when they show up uninvited. Many people believe emotions just *happen* in the moment, as if they spring out of nowhere like pop-up ads. But here's the truth: Emotions are rarely about *right now*. They're built over time, rooted in past experiences, stored beliefs, and unprocessed patterns.

In leadership and life, this means what looks like an overreaction is usually an overdue reaction.

Let me show you what I mean.

Imagine two men, Ben and Josh, who are stuck in traffic on their way to an important business meeting. They're both introverts. They both love golf.

They both scored the same on the Myers-Briggs. They even both hate being late. On paper, they're basically the same person. But here's what happens.

Ben sighs, turns on a podcast, and uses the delay to catch up on industry news. He calls his business partner, explains the situation, and resets the expectation calmly.

Josh? Not so calm. He starts weaving between lanes, muttering under his breath, snapping at other drivers. He calls his business partner and insists she hold the meeting until he gets there because *he has to be there.*

Same traffic. Same meeting. Two completely different responses. Why?

Because of emotional buildup.

What you didn't see is what happened to Josh before he got in the car. The last time he missed a meeting, his partner ran it without him, and it went off the rails. He told himself that wouldn't happen again. He planned to leave early, but that morning, he discovered his teenage son had borrowed the tire-changing tools and left them somewhere mysterious (as teenagers tend to do). So Josh was delayed, covered in oil, flustered, and walking into traffic with a head full of pressure and a body full of tension.

Josh wasn't just reacting to the traffic. He was reacting to everything that came *before* the traffic. His trigger wasn't the delay; it was the fear of another leadership failure.

This is how emotional triggers work.

They don't show up with a name tag or calendar invite. They show up in our reactions: quick, sharp, and disproportionate to the moment. And while pausing helps us regain composure, it doesn't *resolve* the trigger. That's the next level of mindset work: learning to identify what's really behind the emotion.

In neuroscience, this is called **emotional tagging.** Your brain doesn't just store events, but the emotions connected to them as well. When a current moment resembles a past pain point, your brain lights up the same neural pathway, as if to say, *Hey, remember when this went badly last time? Brace yourself!* That's why your reaction feels urgent, even if the situation doesn't objectively justify it.

According to Dr. Lisa Feldman Barrett, a leading researcher in affective neuroscience, emotions aren't hardwired responses; they're predictions your brain makes based on past experiences. The emotion you feel now is your brain guessing what's about to happen based on what happened before.

So, what looks like a meltdown in the moment is usually a backlog of emotions that never got processed. This is why the pause matters. It gives you the power to stop the spiral before it becomes your story. But awareness alone isn't enough. To truly shift your mindset, you've got to go deeper. You've got to recognize what's underneath the reaction. You have to recognize the root cause.

Why We Get Triggered

If you read the story of Ben and Josh and were thinking, "Get a grip, Josh. It's not that bad," perhaps you should turn that inspection inward. Have you ever found yourself reacting sharply to a comment, a decision, or even a facial expression, almost before you realize what's happening? That moment of emotional charge, when something in your environment causes a surge of frustration, fear, anxiety, or even defensiveness, is the type of trigger Josh experienced. While you might not wave angry gestures at someone in traffic, you might get defensive when a co-worker wants to see your work or anxious when you have to go into a meeting. We all have things that trigger us, but we don't have to let the triggers run the show.

Triggers are deeply tied to how the brain forms habits and perceives threats. To shift into a resilient mindset, you must first become aware of what sets off their fixed, reactive responses. Understanding the science behind this is key to changing it.

Inside the Brain

Our brains are hardwired for efficiency and protection. Every day, we're bombarded with countless stimuli, which our brains automate as much as possible. Basically, our brain tries to make life easier for us, so we don't have to think deeply about everything we experience. It creates mental shortcuts based on past experiences, which is how habits are formed. When a similar situation arises, the brain then retrieves a familiar pattern to save energy and respond quickly.

The same applies to emotional reactions. For example, if you grew up in a highly competitive environment where failure wasn't tolerated, your brain may associate constructive feedback with judgment and rejection. You might also try to win others over with your performance since your brain connected positive results with love and acceptance. So, when someone offers a suggestion at work, your brain sounds the alarm and triggers defensiveness, signaling that you're not safe and you're losing their love. Even though the current situation is completely safe, your brain can't necessarily spot the difference due to the patterns it has already created.

When this happens, the amygdala hijack takes place (check the previous chapter for a recap if needed). Your logic and reasoning get pushed out the window and are replaced with fight, flight, or freeze. That's why triggers lead to irrational and unhelpful reactions. It's actually because your brain is doing what it was created to do: protect you.

Recognize the Root Cause

If the pause is the doorway to mindset change, then recognizing your emotional triggers is what helps you walk through it with intention. Most people don't explore why they react the way they do because they're too busy cleaning up the mess afterward. But leadership isn't about damage control. It's about self-awareness. The email isn't your trigger. The traffic jam isn't your trigger. The teammate who missed the deadline? Also not your trigger. What triggers you is the meaning your brain assigns to those moments. Maybe it hits your fear of being dismissed, your belief that you're unsupported, or the story that if you're not in control, everything falls apart. Chances are, that belief didn't start today. That's why two people can face the same situation and walk away with completely different emotional responses. One feels fine. The other spirals. It's not the situation. It's the story underneath it.

So, how do you find yours? Start with patterns. Notice what consistently spikes your emotions, which environments or people put you on edge, or where your reaction feels bigger than the moment itself. That's your signal. That's your brain saying, "Look here!" Your triggers aren't flaws. They're clues. They point to the beliefs, fears, and expectations you've absorbed over time, usually without realizing it. But once you see them, you get to decide: *Do I keep reacting, or do I rewrite the story?* That's the shift. From autopilot to awareness. From reacting to leading. And when you do this, you don't just change how you lead yourself, you change how others experience you. That's not woo woo fluff. That's power.

The Many Faces of Triggers

Triggers can come from many places. They're not confined to your past or loud noises in the office. By learning to recognize different types of triggers, you can begin to understand your emotional response more clearly and with compassion. You'll begin to see where your triggers come from and why they are causing so much reactivity. Remember, be kind to yourself. All of this is your brain trying to keep you safe. The best way to move forward is to create a safe space for yourself where triggers are viewed objectively and not as something forbidden. Let's break down some common categories of triggers that may be shaping your mindset and behaviors.

Environmental Factors

Your environment speaks, sometimes louder than words. Noise, clutter, chaos, or even someone's unspoken energy can send subtle cues to your brain that something is off. Maybe it's the hum of a tense boardroom, the open plan office with zero privacy, or stepping into a space where conflict often erupts. Suddenly, you're edgy, distracted, or emotionally flooded, and you can't quite explain why. That's not just a mood; that's wiring. Your brain is constantly scanning for signs of safety or the lack of it. A messy space, a sarcastic tone, or just too much happening at once can quietly flip your system into defense mode. You may not realize it, but your leadership presence just left the building. You don't need candles, a yoga mat, or whale sounds to lead well, but you do need awareness. Recognizing environmental triggers isn't about controlling every room you walk into. It's about understanding and being aware when your nervous system is being hijacked so you can regulate instead of react. When you stop absorbing the chaos and start anchoring yourself, your leadership becomes the calm in the room, not the echo of the noise.

The Emotional Backpack You Are Wearing

We all carry an invisible backpack into work every day, loaded with financial stress, relationship tension, family drama, health concerns, or just that vague "I'm not okay and I don't know why" feeling. You may think you're keeping it together, but your body knows what it's holding, and when pressure builds internally, even minor external stressors can trigger major reactions. You might find yourself snapping at your team, zoning out in meetings, or overcompensating with perfectionism, not because of what's happening *at* work, but because of what you brought *into* work.

Knowing what's in your backpack doesn't mean unloading it at the office door, but it *does* mean noticing when the weight is too much and taking responsibility before it spills out sideways. This kind of awareness doesn't just build emotional intelligence. It protects your team from emotional shrapnel.

Too Loud, Too Bright, Too Much

Sometimes, the problem isn't emotional. It's environmental input on overdrive. Sensory overload happens when your brain is flooded with more stimulation than it can reasonably process. Think buzzing notifications, fluorescent lighting, back-to-back meetings, overlapping conversations, the smell of burnt coffee wafting through the office, and someone's overly enthusiastic perfume trailing behind them like a cloud. This isn't a crisis. It's just a Tuesday morning for the modern leader. But in these moments, your capacity to think clearly and regulate emotions tanks. You may snap, shut down, or completely zone out, not because you're weak, but because your system is overwhelmed and trying to protect you the only way it knows how.

And here's the tricky part: Everyone's threshold is different, and it changes day to day. What feels fine on Monday might feel unbearable by Thursday.

Recognizing sensory overload isn't about being high maintenance, it's about being self-aware. When you know your limits, you can protect your clarity, preserve your presence, and create space to reset before re-engaging.

Because resilient leaders don't just power through. They *notice* and adjust.

When The Past Crashes Your Meeting

Triggers don't always come from the present moment. Sometimes, they're echoes carried in from experiences you thought you left behind. A toxic boss, a broken relationship, a public failure, or a childhood wound you've tucked neatly away. One comment, one glance, one familiar tone, and suddenly, your brain sounds the alarm.

That's not overreacting. That's your nervous system trying to protect an old version of you.

Post-traumatic triggers aren't always dramatic. Often, they're subtle, but the emotional intensity feels huge. You're not responding to *this* situation. You're responding to *that* memory.

The key is self-awareness. When you understand where your emotional reaction is coming from, you can lead the moment instead of being led by it.

Healing doesn't mean the trigger disappears. It means it no longer dictates your response. And in leadership, learning to lead through old wounds without re-inflicting them? That's where real power begins.

You Are Not Spiraling, You Are Just Hungry

Not all triggers come from childhood trauma or emotional wounds. Sometimes, you just need a sandwich. Or a nap. Or both. Sleep deprivation and poor nutrition don't just mess with your energy; they compromise your ability to think clearly, regulate emotions, and make solid decisions. You're more likely to snap at your team, doubt yourself, or spiral into worst-case scenarios when your body is running on fumes. The brain reads fatigue and hunger as threats, so even small stressors can feel enormous when your system is under-resourced. This isn't a mindset problem; it's biology. If everything feels personal and overwhelming, pause and check in: *Am I actually just exhausted? Have I eaten something with real nutrients today?* You can't lead well from an empty tank. Take care of your physical needs, and your emotional intelligence will thank you for it. Strong leadership doesn't ignore the body. It works with it.

The Pressure Cooker In a Suit

Some triggers don't come from the past. They come from the office. Work is one of the sneakiest trigger factories out there. Deadlines pile up, priorities shift by the hour, and the pressure to perform is constant, but nobody talks about it. It builds fast and quietly. You don't even notice it at first, but then you're waking up at 3 a.m. thinking about a client email, or snapping at your team over something small. That's not just stress. That's your nervous system hitting its limit.

When the pressure to deliver becomes a trigger, your brain flips into survival mode. You go into overdrive, or you shut down. You avoid risk, delay decisions, or try to control everything because it feels safer than failing. That's not leadership. That's self-protection. High expectations aren't the enemy. The real problem is pretending the pressure isn't affecting you. The fix isn't quitting or scaling back. It's learning to pause, check in, and lead yourself through the heat, because peak performance doesn't come from avoiding pressure. It comes from managing it. And that, right there, is where real leadership earns its edge.

How to Identify Your Triggers

Identifying your triggers is like putting batteries in a flashlight when you're stuck in a dark room. It might not be the final step to seeing clearly, but without it, you're just bumping into walls and guessing what's in front of you. When you know your triggers, you stop getting swept away by emotional reactions and start leading with clarity and control. But before we dive into identifying them, say this out loud: Identifying triggers is not about judgment; it's about awareness. The goal isn't to beat yourself up for the things that set you off. The goal is to understand them. Because with awareness comes the power to choose differently. With judgment, all you get is shame and shutdown. If you want to lead others with clarity, consistency, and confidence, you have to learn how to lead yourself first, and that starts with knowing what's happening beneath the surface when you react. Emotional triggers don't just appear out of nowhere. They leave a trail. They show up in your body, in your thoughts, and in the tone you use when you say "I'm fine" and absolutely do not mean it. Those clues are gold. When you learn to recognize them, you can start responding instead of reacting. Here's a simple step-by-step process leaders can use to uncover what's really driving their reactions, because self-awareness isn't just a soft skill. It's a leadership superpower.

Step 1: Identifying Your Reaction

The first step to identifying your triggers starts with the moment of impact. When something unsettles you, move to pause, then ask yourself: *What am I feeling right now?* Emotions like anger, frustration, embarrassment, sadness, or anxiety are often signals that you've been triggered. But sometimes, it shows up more subtly, like withdrawal, avoidance, defensiveness, or even sarcasm. During this step, pay attention to physical symptoms. Your body often knows you're triggered before your mind does. Common physical cues include:

- A racing heart
- Tightness in your chest
- Shallow breathing
- Sweaty palms
- Tension in your jaw and shoulders
- A knot in your stomach

These physical responses are part of the body's natural stress response system. They are cues that something's not right. When you learn to notice them early, you gain a chance to interrupt the reactive loop.

Step 2: Consider What Led to the Feelings

Once you've acknowledged how you felt, take a step and ask yourself: *What was happening just before this emotion showed up?* Then, ask yourself further questions, such as:

- Who was I talking to?
- What was said or done?
- Was there a tone, facial expression, or action that sparked discomfort?
- Was I already tired, hungry, or stressed before this happened?

This step requires curiosity. You're not blaming anyone, you're simply trying to understand the sequence of events. Think of it as emotional detective work. Sometimes the trigger is obvious, and other times it's subtle.

Step 3: Look for Patterns

The real power comes when you begin to connect the dots. Emotional triggers tend to follow patterns, and when you spot them, you can begin to shift them. Ask yourself these questions to help identify triggers:

- Do certain people or situations consistently trigger me?

- Are there specific themes that make me feel defensive, anxious, or unworthy (e.g., being ignored, not having control, receiving feedback)?

- Is there a time of day or context where I'm more sensitive or reactive (e.g., right after a long meeting, when I'm under pressure)?

- Do I have a strong reaction to specific words, tones, or environments?

Recognizing your emotional patterns allows you to pause before the reaction takes over. You move from reacting out of habit to responding with intention.

Mindset Reflection

Before we move on to step three of the MINDSET Framework, it's time for a little practical adventure. Over the next few days, I want you to use the trigger tracking template to reflect on any moment that sparks a strong reaction. The more consistently you journal, the more clearly you'll begin to see the patterns behind your triggers.

Date and Time:	
What happened? Describe the situation briefly. Who was involved? What was said or done?	*Example: I received unexpected critical feedback during the team meeting.*
What did I feel in that moment? Label your emotions. Try to go deeper than just "mad" or "upset."	*Example: Embarrassed, frustrated, defensive.*
What physical sensations did I notice? Tune into your body. Where did you feel the reaction physically?	*Example: Tight chest, flushed face, tense shoulders.*
What happened just before I felt triggered? Was there a specific word, tone, action, or situation that preceded the emotion?	*Example: My manager used a sarcastic tone while commenting on my idea.*

What story did my mind immediately tell me? This helps begin the *name the thought* step. What belief or assumption came up?	*Example: They don't value my input. I'm not good enough to lead this project.*
What was my response? How did I act, speak, or react in that moment?	*Example: I went quiet, avoided eye contact, and didn't share any other ideas.*
Was my response aligned with my values? Did I respond in a way that reflects who I want to be as a leader?	*Example: Yes or No. Why?.*
What could I do differently next time? Identify one way you could pause, reflect, and respond more intentionally.	*Example: Take a breath, remind myself of my strength, ask a clarifying question.*

Chapter 6

N—Name the Thought

*Your leadership grows when you stop trying to prove yourself
and start showing up for your team just the way you are.*

– Sally Allen

Let's do a quick recap of the MINDSET Framework so far. You hit a moment of overwhelm and instead of letting it own you, you chose to **move to pause**. That alone deserves a slow clap. Then, you identified the trigger behind the emotional spike (we call that self-leadership). Now, it's time to meet the next game-changing step: **naming the thought**.

Why does naming the thought matter?

Because when you name a thought, you create distance. It's no longer swirling around inside you like a tornado. It's on the table. You can look at it, challenge it, and make a better choice. Left unnamed, that same thought can hijack your peace, your leadership presence, and your sense of clarity. But when you name it, you disarm it.

Remember earlier when I told you about how I pushed myself to face my fear of water and learn to swim? Well, what I didn't tell you then was how

I first reacted when I walked into the pool area and saw that there were exclusively children learning. I clutched my gym bag and made a beeline right back to my car.

Cue emotional chaos: embarrassment, fear, shame. Thoughts like, *You don't belong here*, *You're going to look ridiculous*, *What were you thinking?* And in that moment, I seriously considered giving up on the whole idea. I told myself I could live without swimming. It wasn't that important, right? But I caught myself. I moved to pause, identified the trigger, and then I named the thought.

The loudest one was: *Everyone is going to judge me and think I'm a joke.*

As soon as I named it, the drama deflated. Saying the thought out loud (yes, even just to myself) gave me the clarity I needed. The kids weren't judging me. The instructors weren't keeping score. The parents weren't going to mock me. If anything, people are usually rooting for the underdog, cheering them on. I was trapped in a story I had made up.

Now, saying that thought out loud didn't instantly turn me into a backstroke champion, but it *was* the moment I stopped spiraling. I got curious instead of reactive, and I was able to decide my next move from a place of leading my mind, instead of my mind leading me. That's the power of this next step in the mindset process.

In this chapter, we're going to talk about **how to name the thought**, the different types of thoughts that tend to trip you up the most, and how to call them out before they call the shots.

Because once you name the thought, you stop being ruled by it.

The Importance of Thought Labeling

This is one of the most overlooked steps in mindset work and ironically, one of the most powerful. No journaling marathons. No mental gymnastics. Just this: **Give your thought a name**.

That's it.

This is what we call *thought labeling* (Segal et al., 2002). It's the practice of consciously recognizing and naming the thoughts that pass through your mind, especially when emotions are running high. Think of it like stepping outside yourself for a second to watch your internal dialogue like it's playing on a screen. You're not judging, fixing, or overthinking (Kabat-Zinn, 1990). You're just naming what's there.

Instead of spiraling with, *I'm going to fail at this,* you pause and say, *I'm having the thought that I'm going to fail at this.*

Sounds small. But that shift? It's massive, because now, you're not *inside* the thought, you're looking *at* it. And when you create that space between you and your inner monologue, you create room to challenge it, shift it, or simply not act on it.

Here's the mindset truth: **Thoughts aren't facts**. They're interpretations. Predictions. Narratives your brain generates based on past experience and current pressure. Often without your permission. Labeling your thoughts won't silence them, but it does strip them of their power, and that's where transformation begins. So no, this isn't fluff. This is next-level self-awareness.

Ready to stop letting your thoughts boss you around? Good. Let's name them.

Why Thought Labeling is Important in the Rewiring Process

Here's the problem with a rigid mindset: It rarely gets questioned. The thoughts it produces tend to sound factual, logical, and even familiar. So instead of challenging them, we accept them. We internalize them. And over time, we build our identity around them. Thoughts like:

- I'm not good at this.

- They don't respect me.

- I always mess this up.

Left unchecked, these thoughts stop being thoughts and become beliefs. And those beliefs begin shaping how you lead, how you show up, and what you assume is possible. Your inner dialogue becomes your default compass, quietly guiding every decision, interaction, and interpretation.

That's why **thought labeling is so critical to mindset rewiring**. It disrupts the cycle. When you name a thought, you create space between stimulus and response. You separate fact from feeling, belief from fear. You're no longer reacting from conditioning. You're observing with clarity. And here's where real power enters the picture: Once you name the thought, you get to choose.

Do I want to believe this thought and reinforce my rigid mindset? Or do I want to challenge it and rewire how I think, lead, and respond?

Labeling your thoughts doesn't mean you silence the inner critic. It means you stop giving it the mic. Rewiring starts with awareness. Label the thought. Then lead the shift.

Naming the Thought Reduces Its Power Over You

A few months ago, my computer started acting up. Simple tasks like opening a file or clicking a folder suddenly took forever. I'm talking painfully slow. At first, I assumed it was user error or bad Wi-Fi, but after calling for tech support, I found out what was really going on: A massive system update was running quietly in the background. I hadn't seen it, but it was draining all my computer's processing power.

That's exactly how unspoken thoughts operate.

When left unnamed, they run silently in the background of your mind, eating up all your processing power. You're reacting, second-guessing, spiraling, but you don't know why. Until you stop, scan the system, and name the thought.

That moment of awareness? That's when the power shifts.

In clinical psychology, this is known as *cognitive diffusion*, a technique from Acceptance and Commitment Therapy (ACT) that teaches you to create distance between yourself and your thoughts (Hayes et al., 1990). Instead of being entangled in the narrative, you observe it. You choose how to respond.

Thought labeling interrupts the spiral. It allows you to say, "That's just a thought, not a command", and as a leader, this is a non-negotiable skill. It's how you stay steady under pressure, respond with clarity, and lead from intention, not reactivity.

You can't control every thought. But you can absolutely choose which ones you follow.

Examples of Thought Labeling

Let's be real: Naming or labeling thoughts can sound a lot simpler than it actually is. When your emotions are running high and your brain is yelling *Just leave! This is too much!"*(or, say, trying to talk you out of learning how to swim), creating distance from that internal noise can feel nearly impossible. Emotions blur clarity, they amplify drama, and in the middle of all that mental chaos, it's hard to name the thought, especially if you don't even know what the options are.

So, if you're wondering how you're meant to label something when you've never been taught the categories, you're in luck. The next section is here to help you put language to the internal swirl. We'll look at common unhelpful thought patterns leaders face and how to label them so you can stop reacting, start leading, and take your power back.

Negative Self-Talk

What it is:

Negative self-talk is dialogue that's critical, discouraging, or shaming. These thoughts often attack your worth or ability.

Examples:

- I'm terrible at this.
- I'm not leadership material.
- I always mess things up.

How to label it:

"I'm having the thought that I'm not capable. That is a self-critical thought, and not a fact."

Why it matters:

Negative self-talk is one of the fastest ways to stay stuck in a rigid mindset. It's like having a bully living rent-free in your brain, one who constantly reminds you of your flaws, doubts your decisions, and undermines your worth. And here's the kicker: You eventually start to believe it!

Ask yourself this: Would you stay friends with someone who talked to you the way your inner critic does? I doubt it.

When left unchecked, that internal dialogue erodes self-trust. It creates emotional friction and strips away your self-worth. Over time, you don't just hear the voice, you *become* it. But when you label the thought by saying, "This is a self-critical thought," you hit pause. You interrupt the loop, and that space allows you to replace harshness with honesty, criticism with curiosity, and judgment with something far more effective: self-leadership.

Because resilient leaders don't self-sabotage. They self-correct.

Catastrophizing

What it is:

Catastrophizing is when your brain turns a paper cut into a near-death experience. Something small goes wrong, and instead of seeing it for what it is, your mind takes the express train to Worst Case Scenario Land. A late email becomes "I'm getting fired." A small dip in sales becomes "The whole business is collapsing."

It is not that you are dramatic for fun. Your brain is wired for threat detection, and catastrophizing happens when that system goes into overdrive. The problem is, this mental habit burns energy, increases stress, and keeps you from responding with clarity.

The antidote is to catch it early. Name it: "I'm catastrophizing." Pull the lens back and ask, "What is the most likely outcome here?" Think of your mind like a playlist. When the doom track starts playing, recognize it, skip it, and choose something grounded instead. Grounded people do not live on recycled fear. They stay present and intentional, even when an old breakup song starts on repeat. Just recognize it. And choose a new track.

Examples:

- If I mess up this presentation, I'll lose all credibility and never get another chance to speak in front of leadership.
- If I'm not perfect, they'll finally see I'm a fraud, and everything I've worked for will unravel.

How to label it:

"I'm having a catastrophic thought. My brain is trying to protect me by imagining the worst possible scenario."

Why it matters:

It comes as no surprise to learn that catastrophizing fuels anxiety and indecision. When you name the thought, it will help you to remain grounded in what's *actually* happening, instead of having sleepless nights about what *might* happen.

Stop "Shoulding" All Over Yourself

What it is:

"Should" is sneaky. It wears a professional face and sounds like high standards, but underneath? It's all rigidity, guilt, and self-imposed pressure dressed up as leadership.

These aren't growth-oriented thoughts. They're inner ultimatums. And they usually trace back to perfectionism, fear of disappointing others, or a deep need for control. The problem? "Should" statements don't motivate, they shame.

When you notice yourself spiraling in shoulds, pause. Label it. *This is a "should" thought.* That small shift moves you out of self-blame and back into agency.

Because leadership isn't about being perfect, it's about being present. And the truth is, *should* isn't strategy. It's a story.

Examples:

- I should always be confident.
- They should know better.
- I shouldn't feel this way.
- They should have achieved this by now.

How to label it:

"That's a should thought, a sign I might be holding unrealistic expectations. I'm putting pressure on myself (or my team) with this thought."

Why it matters:

"Should" statements don't drive performance; they drive burnout. When you constantly measure yourself or your team against internal expectations like *I should be further along* or *They should know better by now,* you create pressure without progress.

The danger is this: "should" implies someone is already failing. Read that again. It skips collaboration and jumps straight to judgment, and over time, it erodes your morale and the morale of those around you.

Leadership isn't about holding invisible scorecards. It's about setting intentional, realistic expectations that support growth. So, when a thought shows up wrapped in "should," pause and label it. Ask yourself: *Is this standard helpful, or just habitual? Is it based on strategy or perfectionism dressed as accountability?*

Labeling helps you shift from criticism to clarity and helps you stop shaming yourself or others in an attempt to achieve excellence.

Labeling Others and Mind Reading

What it is:

Labeling others or assuming you know what they're thinking? That's not clarity, it's mental shortcutting with a confidence problem.

Mind reading and labeling are fast but rarely accurate. You don't have psychic abilities, so stop guessing. Choose objectivity over assumption, and instead of reacting to an imagined storyline, pause and label the distortion. That simple act breaks the loop. I know it's easier to make up a story than to face the real issue, but avoiding the truth never leads to growth.

Examples:

- They think I'm incompetent.
- My team hates me.
- He always gets what he wants because he is the favorite.
- They are always judging me.

How to label it:

"That's a mind-reading thought. I'm assuming I know what they're thinking, but the truth is I don't. I'm assigning a label without knowing their story, and that's not fair or helpful.

Why it matters:

Labeling and mind-reading thoughts quietly erode trust. They lead to miscommunication, defensiveness, and unnecessary tension, especially in leadership, where clarity is non-negotiable.

These thoughts often mask fear or disappointment, as it feels safer to assume someone's against you than to consider their feedback might be valid. But that assumption costs you connection.

When you name the thought, saying, *I'm mind reading right now,* you stop treating guesswork as fact. You step out of the story and into curiosity. From there, you get to choose: *Do I engage with bias, or with fairness?* One keeps you stuck. The other keeps you in your power.

Overgeneralizing

What it is:

Overgeneralizing takes one bad experience and turns it into a rule. *That meeting bombed, so I'm a terrible speaker. They didn't like my idea, no one ever does.* It's your brain turning a single data point into a universal truth. This mindset shuts down growth. It makes you think, *If nothing ever changes, why bother trying?*

But here's the truth: One bad experience is not your track record. It's a moment in your life, not your entire life. Overgeneralizing is a distortion, not a diagnosis. When you label the thought, you interrupt the spiral and stop writing future chapters based on a single page.

Leadership requires perspective. Label the lens and rewrite the narrative.

Examples:

- I froze during the Q&A after my presentation. Everyone probably thinks I'm incompetent.

- I wasn't included in that strategy meeting. They must not see me as important to the team.

How to label it:

"That's an overgeneralization. I'm basing a broad conclusion on one moment. This is one event, not the whole story."

Why it matters:

Overgeneralizing locks you into a mindset that treats failure as permanent and progress as pointless. One setback suddenly becomes a sweeping conclusion: *I always mess this up. It never works out.* That mindset doesn't just distort reality. It drains motivation.

Labeling the thought separates the event from your identity. You're not a failure, you're just *experiencing* a setback, and once you give the thought a name, you shift from being inside the spiral to observing it. That's where growth begins: when you see clearly, reflect honestly, and decide how to move forward without dragging the past into your future.

Thought Labeling Exercises

Thought labeling isn't just a mindset shift. It's a leadership skill. And like any skill worth developing, it takes intention and consistent practice. You're training your brain to move from automatic reactions to conscious responses that are aligned with your values.

The exercises that follow are designed to help you build your mental muscles. Simple, practical, and deeply effective, they'll help you shift from reacting impulsively to responding with grounded awareness.

One quick note before we begin: Mastery isn't about getting it perfect. It's about repetition. Every time you pause to name a thought, you're rewiring your mental pathways and reinforcing your power to lead yourself well. You don't need to control every thought. You just need to know how to lead them.

Write It Down or Say It Out Loud

When you say a thought out loud or write it down, you move it out of your head and into the light. That act alone creates distance, and distance brings clarity. Ever vented to a coworker and solved the problem mid-rant? That's not magic, it's how the brain processes.

Externalizing your thoughts interrupts the rumination loop. It lets you observe instead of absorb. When you *name* the thought as you express it, you take it off autopilot and start leading with intention instead of emotion. Insight doesn't come from silence. It comes from seeing.

Be Specific

Unhelpful thoughts thrive in vagueness. The more general they are, the more power they hold. "This is a disaster" feels overwhelming because it's undefined. But specificity cuts through the noise and puts you back in control.

When you push deeper—*Why am I thinking this? What exactly am I afraid of? Who am I worried about?*—you force your brain to clarify its case. That clarity weakens the emotional punch. Instead of spiraling with *This is a mess,* try: *I'm having the thought that this deadline feels impossible, and I'm afraid I'll come off as unreliable to my boss.*

Now you've got something to work with. Specific thoughts can be evaluated, reframed, and led. Vague thoughts just spiral, and in leadership, vague thinking costs too much. So name it. Define it. Then decide what you want to do with it. If your mindset feels overwhelming, ask better questions. Clarity isn't just calming, it's empowering.

Consider the Consequences of the Thought

Let's recap.

- You've paused.
- You've identified the trigger.
- You've labeled the thought.

Now it's time to consider its impact. Ask yourself: *What does this thought cost me emotionally? How does it shape the way I show up? What might happen if I keep thinking this every day?*

For example: *I'm having the thought that I'm not cut out for leadership.* If that thought drives your decisions, you might stop speaking up, stop growing, and eventually stop believing in yourself.

This step is about connecting the dots, not just between thoughts and feelings, but between thoughts and outcomes. Once you see the ripple effect clearly, change becomes possible.

Now, let's move into the Mindset Reflections and put it all together.

Mindset Reflection

As always, it's time to put what you've learned into practice. Thought labeling only becomes powerful when you use it in real moments, not just when it sounds good on paper. To help you build the habit, I've created a simple, journal-style worksheet you can use to walk through the process step by step. Use it anytime you feel emotionally triggered, stuck in a negative loop, or just want to sharpen your self-awareness. This isn't busywork, it's brain training. The more you practice, the more automatic clarity becomes.

Date/Time:

1. What happened?

Briefly describe the situation or event.

_____
_____
_____
_____

2. How did you feel?

Write down the emotions you noticed (e.g., anxious, angry, sad, ashamed):

_____
_____
_____
_____

Did you notice any physical symptoms (e.g., racing heart, shallow breath, tense shoulders)?

_____
_____
_____
_____

3. What were you thinking?

Write the raw thought that came up for you:

_____
_____
_____
_____

4. Label the thought
Use this prompt: "I'm having the thought that…"

_____
_____
_____
_____

Now identify the type of thought it is by using this Thought Type Checklist:

☐ Negative self-talk

☐ Catastrophizing

☐ "Should" statement

☐ Labeling/mind reading

☐ Over Generalizing

☐ Other: _____

Thought Labeling Statement:

_____

_____

_____

_____

5. Be specific
What exactly are you afraid will happen? Who is involved? What's the worst case you're imagining?

_____

_____

_____

_____

6. What is the impact of this thought?
How does it make you feel?

_____

_____

_____

_____

What actions might you take if you believe it?

_____

_____

_____

_____

What long-term effect could it have if repeated?

_____
_____
_____
_____

7. Reflection notes

_____
_____
_____
_____

Chapter 7

D—Dissect the Belief

When you shift from controlling everything to influencing what matters, you step into real leadership.

–Sally Allen

Most limiting beliefs and rigid mindsets aren't built on truth. They're built on assumptions, outdated fears, and old narratives we've never stopped to challenge. We jump to conclusions with little to no evidence, then build our confidence (or lack of it) on top of shaky ground.

In the last step, you learned how to name your thoughts. Now, it's time to go deeper. This step isn't just about awareness, it's about investigation. It's where you ask: *Is this thought actually true? Or is it a leftover script I never meant to memorize?*

To dissect a belief means to slow down and get under the hood of it. What's really going on beneath the thought you just labeled? What triggered it? Where did it come from? And more importantly, does it still belong in your mental operating system?

But let's be real: You can't dissect what you haven't first paused to name. If you skip straight to questioning without creating emotional distance, you'll end up defending the thought instead of investigating it. Objectivity only comes after self-awareness.

Once you're in that clear headspace, the next step is to challenge the thought. Ask: *Who taught me this? What experience formed it? What evidence supports or completely disproves it?*

Here's what I know: Most of the time, our loudest thoughts are our least reliable ones.

For years, I believed I wasn't qualified to run my own business, let alone write a book on mindset and leadership. That was a job for other people, "real" experts. I didn't even stop to question that narrative. It just ran quietly in the background, shaping how I showed up (or didn't).

But the day I asked, "Is this actually true?" was the day the belief started to unravel.

You see, unchallenged thoughts don't just stay in your head. They shape your choices, your voice, your growth. Dissecting the thought isn't about proving yourself wrong. It's about giving yourself the chance to lead from truth, not fear.

Becoming a Detective

Your mind is powerful, but let's be honest, it's not always accurate. I know, shocker, right? As we discussed in previous chapters, you have thousands of thoughts a day, and many of them aren't based on logic or truth. They're running on emotion, outdated wiring, or whatever narrative your brain defaulted to years ago. If you agree with every single thought that pops up, it's like reading every headline on the internet and assuming the worst without bothering to read the full story. You get drama, not data.

Just because a thought is loud doesn't mean it's right.

Take a thought like, *I am a failure.* It might *feel* true when you're overwhelmed or under pressure, but is it? Is it really? That's why dissecting your thoughts is a non-negotiable, not just for your mental clarity, but for your leadership credibility.

When you become the detective of your own mind, your job is to investigate, not just accept. Your tool? Evidence. Ask yourself:

- What facts support this belief?
- What facts directly contradict it?
- Am I interpreting this with objectivity or from a reactive place?
- Would I ever say this out loud to someone I respect or care about?

These questions help you break out of the loop of blind acceptance and move into informed awareness. You shift from swimming in fear-based assumptions to anchoring yourself in grounded truth.

Within the context of leadership, that shift is everything, because here's the reality: Your beliefs dictate how you lead. If you believe you're not capable, you'll hesitate. If you believe people can't grow, you'll micromanage instead of develop. But if you dissect and reframe those beliefs, you create space for new possibilities. For yourself. For your team. For your vision.

Thoughts show up automatically. That's just how the brain works. But beliefs? Beliefs are formed through repetition and agreement. If you keep nodding along to the wrong ones, you reinforce a mindset that shrinks you. But if you pause, question, and examine them with intention, you break the pattern and start building beliefs that align with who you're becoming, not who you used to be.

Core Beliefs vs Surface Thoughts

Did you know that not all thoughts carry the same weight? Some are fleeting, like clouds drifting across the sky, influenced by mood, caffeine, or the playlist you picked this morning. Others? They're deeply rooted, quietly steering the ship from below deck. These are your core beliefs. Knowing the difference between the two is essential if you want to rewire your mindset and lead with intention, not instinct.

Surface thoughts are the automatic chatter that runs in the background. They're reactive, emotionally charged, and often as dramatic as a soap opera monologue. Thoughts like, *I'll never figure this out,* or, *Everyone's ahead of me.* Left unchecked, they start to feel like truth, but here's the kicker: Many of these surface thoughts are just echoing deeper core beliefs. That's when the plot thickens.

Core beliefs are the deeply embedded truths you hold about yourself, others, and the world. Formed over time through childhood experiences, culture, and relationships, they operate silently, like your phone's operating system. You don't always see them, but everything runs through them.

Here's why this matters: When you confuse a surface thought for a core belief, you give temporary emotion permanent power. Not every thought deserves a guest room in your brain. Some just need a polite nod and the door. That doesn't mean you judge your thoughts. You observe them like a savvy leader watching how the room is reacting. You pause and ask, *Is this a passing reaction or is it echoing something I've believed for way too long?* That's when your leadership mindset sharpens.

Compare the thought to your values. If your core belief is strong and the thought sounds rigid, you've got your answer. When you reinforce values, you weaken fear. When you chase old beliefs, you reinforce limitations. Every time you believe a thought, whether surface level or deeply rooted, you feed it. So ask yourself: *Am I feeding fear or confidence? Scarcity or strength? Doubt or growth?* You don't have to believe every loud thought. Just the ones that align with who you're becoming.

There have been many times in my life when I had to choose what I wanted to believe about myself: Did I want to continue to feed the negative thoughts based on my past experiences, or did I want to feed a new, positive way of thinking about myself and my abilities? I had to decide that my past would no longer determine my future, but would serve as a positive reminder of how far I've already come. If I could survive all of that, surely I won't allow a simple swimming lesson to take me out, right? But it all came down to a powerful choice, which I then had to confirm over and over again.

Because at the end of the day, your thoughts tell a story. And you get to choose which one you live by.

The Five "Whys" Method

Sometimes a thought feels true simply because we've never slowed down long enough to question it. A statement like "I'm a terrible leader" might hit hard, but intensity doesn't equal accuracy. Most of the time, that thought isn't rooted in fact—it's driven by fear, assumption, or one bad Monday that took up too much space. So, how do we dig deeper and dissect these thoughts in a meaningful way? One powerful tool is the Five "Whys" (Toyota production system, n.d.).

If you've ever spent three minutes with a toddler, you've likely been peppered with questions: "Why is your hair like that? Why don't you have snacks? Why do grown-ups work so much?" Relentless? Yes. But brilliant? Also yes. That same kind of persistence is exactly what rewiring your mindset requires. Instead of brushing off a heavy thought, borrow that childlike curiosity and start asking "Why?" Now do it five times.

Originally used in business and problem solving through the Toyota Production System, the Five "Whys" method helps uncover the root cause behind surface-level issues. It works just as powerfully in the inner world. By asking "Why?" five times, you can trace a reactive or limiting thought back to the core belief driving it.

Here's what it looks like in action:

Surface thought: I don't have the confidence for this promotion.

Why? Because I'm not sure I can handle the responsibilities.

Why? Because I've never led a team at this level before.

Why? Because I've always stayed in support roles and avoided leadership opportunities.

Why? Because I worry I'll fail and let people down.

Why? Because deep down, I believe failure would prove I was never leadership material in the first place.

There it is, the core belief driving the fear and self-doubt. The issue isn't just promotion. It's the deeper story underneath: Failure would prove I was never leadership material. That's the belief we need to work with. That's where real mindset change begins. The Five "Whys" might seem simple, but don't underestimate the power of focused curiosity. When used with intention, this tool moves you from surface-level reactions to root-level awareness. And that's where the rewiring starts.

Truth or Fiction—The Leadership Test

Once you've uncovered the real belief driving your mindset, the one hiding underneath all the surface-level noise, you're standing at a critical moment. You can either keep living from that belief, or you can test it. This is where we move from excavation to evaluation.

Grab your metaphorical magnifying glass and ask yourself the most important leadership question: *Is this actually true or just something I've believed for too long?* Here's your internal truth test:

- Is this belief actually true, or just familiar?
- Would I speak to my employees this way?
- Does this belief help me grow, or does it keep me small?

- What would become possible if I let it go and chose something more empowering?

You don't need to bulldoze the old belief. Just start by questioning its authority. When you bring curiosity instead of shame to the conversation, you start making wiser, more grounded decisions personally and professionally.

This is the mindset shift: You're not at the mercy of every thought or belief that crosses your mind. You get to evaluate, edit, and choose what stays, and when you lead yourself with that kind of clarity, everyone around you feels it.

The Friend Method

When you're stuck in a loop of negative self-talk, you often treat yourself in ways you'd never treat someone else. You're harsher, more critical, and far less forgiving—like that one manager you swore you'd never become. The problem isn't that you lack empathy. It's that you forget to direct it inward.

That's where the Friend Method comes in.

This simple tool helps interrupt the self-critical spiral by asking one question: Would you say this to a friend? If someone you cared about had the same thought or struggle, how would you respond? Would you tell them they're failing, or would you offer perspective, patience, and maybe a hug and a snack?

Chances are, your inner dialogue would soften if you pictured someone else in your shoes.

The Friend Method is about shifting from judgment to wisdom. It helps you access the grounded, compassionate voice that gets drowned out when your rigid mindset takes over. This isn't about coddling. It's about reframing with clarity and care instead of shame and overcorrection.

Empathy creates the space for change. So the next time your inner voice comes in hot, pause and borrow the voice you use with someone you love. That wisdom is already in you. You've just been saving it for everyone else.

Let's change that.

Using the Friend Method

Using the Friend Method is very easy. Next time you're dissecting a thought, and you recognize it as self-critical or limiting, continue to pause and ask yourself the following questions:

1. **Would I say this to someone I care about?** If a friend or family member made a mistake, would you really call them a failure? If they were struggling, would you tell them they're not good enough? Probably not. You'll most likely help them to see the situation from a different perspective, providing them with fresh insight and encouragement to keep going.

2. **How would a friend or loved one respond to me if I shared this thought with them?** Would they say it's hopeless? Or would they remind you of your strengths and potential? Most of the time, a good friend would help you to see past your emotions and view them more objectively. In doing so, they'll help you to keep going instead of giving up entirely.

3. **If a friend were in my exact situation and told me this same thought, how would I respond to them?** What advice, encouragement, or compassion would you offer a friend? Why can't you offer that same kindness to yourself? When you learn to treat yourself as a friend and not an enemy, your mindset will immediately change for the better.

These questions help you hold up your thoughts in a different light. They allow you to see whether they're fair, accurate, or unnecessarily harsh. More often than not, you'll realize you're expecting more from yourself than you would from anyone else. Let's look at an example of what this might look like in a real-life situation.

Negative thought: "I completely lost the room in that strategy meeting. I sounded unsure, and now no one takes me seriously as a leader."

1. **Would you say this to a friend?** No. I'd say, "You had one tough meeting. That doesn't erase your credibility. Leaders grow by learning from moments like this, not avoiding them."

2. **What would a friend say to me?** "You've earned your seat at the table. One moment of doubt doesn't undo everything you've built."

3. **What would I say to a friend who felt this way?** "Let's look at what happened and pull the lesson out of it. This doesn't define you. It prepares you."

By running the thought through the Friend method, the inner dialogue softens. You begin to see the situation from a more balanced, truthful, and growth-oriented perspective.

Putting it Together

So, how does this actually fit into the full framework? Let's walk it through.

Say you're feeling overwhelmed. Not just mildly annoyed but overstimulated, emotionally hijacked, and convinced you're on the verge of dropping all the balls. You've already applied the first few steps: You paused, identified the trigger, and named the thought. Good. That's the awareness phase, and it's essential, but it's not the finish line.

Now you ask the next crucial question: *Is this thought fact or fiction?* Is it 100% true, or is your nervous system just throwing a tantrum in a business suit? To get clarity, dig deeper using the Five "Whys" method. Ask yourself:

Why do I believe this? Then ask again. And again. You're not being annoying, you're being a mindset detective. The truth tends to hide under the first few layers of emotion.

Once you've uncovered the root, you need to pivot to compassion because insight without empathy turns into self-criticism disguised as growth. That's where the Friend Method steps in. Run the thought through that filter and notice how your inner dialogue shifts from ruthless to reasonable. You're still honest, but you stop being cruel in the process.

Finally, take that thought and line it up against your core values. Ask yourself: *Which voice am I reinforcing right now? The one rooted in fear or the one aligned with who I'm becoming?* Every thought feeds something. You get to decide if you're fueling an old pattern or strengthening your leadership mindset.

That's the loop: from reaction to reflection to realignment.

Mindset Reflection

As we wrap up this step, it's time to put it into practice. This exercise will help you walk through the process of identifying a negative thought, digging into its root using the Five "Whys," and then reframing it with the Friend Method. Give yourself 15–20 minutes of uninterrupted time to do this with full focus and honesty.

Step 1: Identify the Thought

Write down a negative thought you've had recently, something that triggered frustration, shame, anxiety, or self-doubt.

_____

_____

_____

Step 2: Dissect With the Five Whys

Ask "Why?" five times to uncover what belief may be driving this thought.

- Why:
- Why:
- Why:
- Why:
- Why:

What belief did you uncover at the root?

_____

_____

_____

Step 3: Challenge With the Friend Method

Now let's shift perspectives and bring self-compassion.

- Would I say this to a friend?

- What would a kind, honest friend say to me?

- If a friend shared this thought with me, how would I respond to them?

Step 4: Determine the Outcome

After all of this, would you consider this thought to be true or based on an assumption?

_____

_____

_____

Bonus Step: Reflections

- What did you learn about yourself through this process?

- How can you remind yourself of this new belief moving forward?

This activity can be repeated any time a limiting belief or negative thought pattern arises. Over time, you'll strengthen your mental muscles of curiosity, compassion, and conscious choice, the hallmarks of a rewired mindset.

Chapter 8

S—Shift Your Perspective

Clarity doesn't come from overthinking; it comes from taking action.
Leaders move first, then refine as they go.

– Sally Allen

You've already come so far. You've learned how to pause, identify your triggers, name your thoughts, and dissect your beliefs. Take a moment to acknowledge the work you've already put in and pat yourself on the back. These aren't just chapters in a book. They are powerful steps in clearing out mental clutter, making room for growth. But here's the truth: Awareness alone doesn't change your mindset. Mindset work doesn't stop at recognizing what's broken. It's about choosing to see it differently. That shift in perception, that moment you decide to reinterpret your situation, your story, or even your own inner dialogue, is the pivot point. It's where growth begins.

Research shows us that behavior change isn't just about knowing what to fix, but about activating it through intentional shifts and small choices that stick. Translation? Insight won't change your life. Action, fueled by a better perspective, will.

Think of it this way: You cleaned out the mental pantry. You tossed the expired stories, the outdated narratives, the beliefs that left you stuck. You even stocked up on better thoughts that are more empowering and more nourishing. But unless you actively *choose* to feed on those better beliefs, the old ones will sneak back in. Perspective is the moment you say, "This thought no longer runs the show."

This chapter is about that exact moment: the pivot from knowing to reframing. From default mode to deliberate thinking. From reacting to choosing. No matter how self-aware you are, if you keep interpreting your experiences through a lens of fear, scarcity, or self-doubt, the outcome won't change. The story doesn't shift unless you do.

So here's your challenge: Don't just acknowledge your old beliefs, replace them. Choose a different lens, one rooted in possibility and resilient thinking. Because when your perspective shifts, so does your strategy, your energy, and your impact.

Transformation doesn't begin when you gain insight. It begins when you see yourself, your challenges, and your capacity through a new lens and then act on it.

Why Shifting Perspective Matters

Your thoughts are the lens. Your mindset is the filter. And your perspective? That's the compass. It determines how you interpret what's in front of you, how you lead through uncertainty, and how you make decisions when it's not just your name on the line.

So what happens when that lens is fogged up with fear, doubt, or scarcity? You shrink your thinking. Your options feel limited. You start playing defense in a game that requires strategy. And here's the kicker: Most of the time, you don't even realize it's happening.

By now, you've already done the heavy lifting. You've named the thought. You've peeled back the layers. You've identified the misalignment between what you're thinking and who you actually are. Now comes the move that changes everything: you shift it.

And no, this isn't mindset fluff. Reframing your perspective is backed by research in Cognitive Behavioral Theory, showing that how we *interpret* an event impacts our emotional and behavioral response more than the event itself. Translation? It's not the situation. It's how you *see* the situation that creates your outcome.

Perspective is power. It's what turns a missed opportunity into a leadership lesson. It's what helps you lead with intention instead of irritation after a meeting that went sideways. The best part? You always have access to it. Even when it doesn't *feel* like a choice, it is. Especially when you're equipped with the right mindset tools.

This step is about reclaiming that choice, because once you realize you don't have to believe every thought that passes through your mind, you stop leading from reaction and start leading from resilience. Your thoughts can either run the meeting, or you can.

Not long ago, I got a call asking me to speak to a group of 25 senior executives at the Aria Hotel in Las Vegas with just two days' notice. No prep materials, no backstory on the audience, no time for overthinking. Just a simple, high-stakes ask: Show up and deliver.

For a moment, my brain panicked. Outwardly, I was calm. But internally? The old script was already playing: *You're not ready. This could go badly. Say no.* That voice didn't come out of nowhere, it came from deeply embedded patterns. Years of limiting beliefs had built a strong mental reflex: don't speak unless every box is checked.

But I knew better. I'd already done the mindset work. I recognized the old pathway, and I had a decision to make: keep walking it or choose something better.

This is what creating a new neural pathway looks like in real life. It's not dramatic. It's not flashy. It's a quiet, internal pivot. One moment, one decision, one powerful reframe: *I've done this before. I don't need perfect. I need presence.*

We covered the neuroscience of this back in Chapter 2—how the brain builds patterns and defaults to them under stress. So here's where that science gets applied. In that moment, I wasn't reciting theory, I was re-routing my internal GPS. I was choosing to lead from capability instead of fear.

That decision didn't just get me through the keynote. It changed how I approach every high-pressure opportunity from then on. It marked a shift in how I trust my preparation, own my voice, and show up for the room, not because I had more time but because I had more awareness. Was I nervous? Yes, but I still showed up.

And that's how new leadership habits are born. You recognize the old response, disrupt it, and choose the path that aligns with who you're becoming, not who you used to be. Choose progress over perfection.

One decision. One upgrade. That's how the brain rewires, and that's how leaders grow.

The Ripple Effect of Perspective

For leaders, shifting your perspective in the face of setbacks isn't just personal. It's cultural. The way you respond to pressure sets the tone for everyone else, because your team isn't just listening to your words, they're studying how you interpret obstacles. When you reframe a failure as feedback or view a detour as redirection, you model what it means to lead with resilience instead of reactivity.

That mindset creates a ripple effect. It signals that innovation matters more than perfection. People stop holding back out of fear of getting it wrong and start leaning into ideas, even if they're messy or incomplete. That's how you get more innovation and less fear of mistakes.

You also shift the energy from blame to ownership. When challenges arise, your team looks for solutions instead of scapegoats. People step up. They collaborate. That's how you get more problem-solving and less blame.

And finally, perspective protects your people. When setbacks are seen as growth points instead of personal failures, the pressure eases. People stop walking on eggshells, and they recover faster. That's how you get more resilience and less burnout.

A leader who sees opportunity in adversity creates a culture where people don't just survive the challenge. They grow because of it. Not because everything goes right, but because the team knows how to reframe what goes wrong.

And that's how you turn a mindset into a movement.

Tools for Shifting Perspective

Shifting your perspective isn't a one-and-done breakthrough. It's a discipline. You're training your brain to choose agility over fear, insight over instinct. That doesn't happen overnight. It's a skill you build one decision at a time. And like any skill worth mastering, you'll need a few solid tools to support the process. The seven tools in the next section are designed to help make perspective-shifting something you do, not just something you hope for. Some of them support this specific step, while others reinforce the mindset muscles you've been building all along.

Reframe Journal

A Reframe Journal is one of the simplest but most effective tools for building mental resilience. It helps you catch unhelpful thoughts as they happen and replace them with something more constructive. Each day, set aside five minutes to reflect on a moment that challenged your mindset.

What triggered you? What story did your brain default to? And what could you choose instead? For each entry, walk through four key questions:

- What happened?
- What was my initial thought?
- What's another way to see this?
- What would the resilient version of me take away from this?

This practice isn't about getting it "right." It's about building a habit of awareness and reframing in real time. Over time, you'll start to recognize the thought patterns that keep showing up, and you'll have the tools to shift them faster. That's how you move from reacting out of habit to responding with intention.

Role Reversal

Your perspective is only as wide as your current lens. When emotions run high or ego takes the wheel, that lens narrows fast. The Role Reversal tool helps you step outside your default view and consider the situation through someone else's eyes, whether that be a team member or even the future version of you who's already grown through this.

Ask yourself: *How would someone I admire handle this? What would my future self say right now?* This simple shift helps you quiet fear, ego, or self-doubt long enough to access a more grounded, compassionate response.

This tool doesn't just expand perspective. It sharpens leadership, builds empathy, deepens emotional intelligence, and helps you lead with values, not just reactions. The more you practice it, the more naturally you'll start to think beyond your own default, and that's where real growth begins.

The Mirror Statement

When pressure hits, your internal tone turns invisible but not harmless. Most people don't realize that their internal tone, the way they speak to themselves, shapes the way they speak to everyone else. That's what makes the Mirror Statement tool so powerful. It helps you regulate the tone of your inner dialogue by bringing it into the light.

Here's how it works: You speak the thought out loud in front of a mirror. *I'm not good enough for this role.* Then you counter it, not with fluff, but with a grounded correction: *That's fear talking. I've done hard things before, and I've shown up under pressure. I can handle this, too.* Hearing your own voice say those words while watching your own face helps you identify whether your tone is harsh, dismissive, or doubtful, and then shift it.

This tool isn't about affirmations. It's about alignment. When your inner voice is supportive instead of critical, your external leadership becomes more composed, more effective, and more human. Research on emotional regulation shows that even subtle shifts in self-talk impact confidence, performance, and how others experience your presence in a room.

The Mirror Statement creates a pause. A moment of recalibration. It teaches you to listen to yourself the way you would a great coach: With clarity, challenge, and compassion.

Because how you speak to yourself sets the tone for how you lead everyone else.

Flip The Script

Your brain loves shortcuts, and unfortunately, one of its favorite defaults is the negative script. *I can't. They probably think I'm incompetent.* These thoughts don't come from logic. They come from conditioning. Script Flipping is the practice of catching that narrative in real time and rewriting it with truth. You don't need to go from *I failed today* to *I'm a genius!* That's not perspective, that's denial. Instead, you shift it to something more grounded: *Today didn't go as planned, but I'm learning and adjusting.*

This is what psychologists call **cognitive reappraisal,** the ability to reinterpret a situation through a more helpful lens (Gross, 1998). Studies in emotional regulation show that people who regularly reframe their thinking are less reactive, more resilient, and better able to navigate stress under pressure.

The more you practice flipping your script, the faster you catch the patterns and the more natural it becomes to lead with clarity instead of self-doubt. Over time, your default internal voice stops sounding like a critic and starts sounding like a coach.

Because mindset isn't just what you believe. It's what you *repeat*.

Time Travel Tool

When emotions run high, perspective runs low. That's why the Time Travel tool is so effective. It gives your mindset the space to breathe. This practice invites you to mentally step out of the urgency of now and ask a powerful question: *How will I wish I had shown up in this moment six months, one year, or five years from now?*

That shift alone can change everything.

Instead of reacting from stress, fear, or frustration, you begin leading from long-range clarity. It helps you re-center on what actually matters: your values, your purpose, and the version of yourself you're working to become. This method is rooted in a research-backed practice known as **episodic future thinking**, which describes the brain's ability to imagine future scenarios using the same systems it uses to recall past experiences (Schacter et al., 2007). Studies show that this type of forward thinking reduces impulsive decision making and increases self-regulation.

This isn't about escaping the present. It's about using the future as a filter. When you consider how this moment fits into the bigger picture, you're far less likely to say something you'll regret, abandon your values, or make a short-term decision that costs you long-term trust.

Time Travel helps you lead with foresight. It brings maturity into moments that could easily unravel. And it reminds you that growth isn't just about pushing through. It's about stepping back, zooming out, and choosing the response your future self will thank you for.

Mindset Anchor

When emotions spike, logic quietly packs its bags and leaves the room. That's where a mindset anchor steps in. It's a short phrase, mantra, or internal pep talk that pulls you out of your mental tailspin and plants your feet back on solid ground. Think of it as a cognitive seatbelt that keeps you from flying off when things get bumpy.

It doesn't have to be poetic. It just has to work. Maybe it's *Respond, don't react.* Or: *Breathe, then lead.* Or my personal favorite: *Not today, I am in control!* These aren't cute captions. They're tools. Saying your anchor out loud (or under your breath if you're mid-meeting and don't want HR involved) engages your **prefrontal cortex,** your brain's command center, and quiets down the amygdala, which would prefer you panic, shut down, or send a regrettable email.

The science behind it is solid. The repetition of a grounding phrase creates a neural association between the words and a calm, focused state. Over time, your brain learns: This phrase = pause + clarity.

The key? Use it often. Write it on a sticky note. Set it as your phone's background. Whisper it to yourself during that "quick sync" that's already gone 45 minutes too long. The more familiar it becomes, the more effective it is.

Staying calm isn't a personality trait. It's a practiced skill. And sometimes, that skill starts with a three-word sentence and a deep breath you actually remember to take.

Gratitude as a Mindset Amplifier

Let's get something straight: Gratitude isn't just a nice idea you pull out at Thanksgiving or when your flight gets upgraded. It's a leadership-level mental tool. A recalibration device. A built-in amplifier for mindset resilience. When challenges hit, gratitude gives your brain something sturdy to hold onto while everything else feels wobbly.

Gratitude doesn't erase the problem, but it does shift the spotlight. Instead of spiraling into what's broken, it brings your attention to what's holding, what's working, and what's still available to you right now. That simple redirection? It disrupts the scarcity loop and makes room for more effective thinking.

Studies in positive psychology (thank you, Dr. Robert Emmons) show that regular gratitude practice increases emotional resilience, reduces cortisol levels, and improves decision making under pressure (2003). Translation: People who practice gratitude don't just feel better, they *lead* better. Because when your brain is trained to recognize what's still good, it's quicker to spot new solutions and slower to collapse into reactivity.

In the middle of a hard moment, pause and ask yourself: *What's one thing I'm grateful for right now?* Not someday. Right now. Or: *What part of this might I appreciate later after the dust settles?* These questions won't fix the situation, but they'll reset your perspective just enough to lead through it.

Want to make it stick? Start small. Three things a day. Keep it in your notes app, on a legal pad, or scribbled in the margins of your to-do list. Doesn't matter where; just make it a habit, especially during the high-stress seasons when your brain is begging for a mental exit ramp. Because here's the truth: A grateful mind doesn't ignore problems. It just refuses to be owned by them.

Mindset Reflection

Let's go back to something I said earlier: Reframing doesn't mean sugarcoating reality. It means learning to see it through a sharper, more empowered lens. When your mindset starts to tighten—when stress, self-doubt, or pressure hijack your clarity—questions become the fastest way to interrupt the spiral and reset your thinking.

But not just any questions. The right ones.

These reflection prompts are designed to challenge tunnel vision, release urgency, and reconnect you to purpose and possibility. Use them in journaling, during quiet reflection, or even mid-meeting when your brain starts writing the wrong script:

- What else could be true here? Break out of all-or-nothing thinking and open yourself to new interpretations of what's actually happening.

- What is this challenge teaching me about myself? Every difficult moment is a mirror. What does it reveal about your growth edge?

- If I were advising my employee, what would I tell them in this situation? Flip the lens. Self-compassion often arrives disguised as wisdom you'd give someone else.

- Will this matter in six months? One year? Zoom out. Regain perspective. Not everything that feels urgent is actually important.

- What's the opportunity in this? Even if it's not obvious yet, train your brain to look for the hidden lesson, redirection, or invitation.

- How can I grow through this, not just get through it? Move from reaction to intention. Leadership doesn't just endure, it evolves.

- What would the future version of me do or believe right now? Step into your future self's mindset. Borrow their clarity when yours feels out of reach.

These aren't feel-good questions. They're practical prompts to rewire how you lead your thoughts. Because the more often you ask better questions, the faster you become someone who sees clearly even when things feel anything but.

Chapter 9

E—Engage in Action

The difference between a struggling leader and a thriving one?
The mindset to see problems as possibilities.

– Sally Allen

A new belief without action is just a motivational poster waiting to fade. Once you've shifted your perspective, you have to engage in action to ensure the new pathways are the ones your brain is taking, or it will default right back to its old neural programming. Your brain doesn't register mindset shifts through insight alone. It needs evidence, and evidence comes from movement.

Don't assume that once the belief shifts, change will magically follow. Because beliefs without behavior are like unlocked doors you never walk through: full of potential, but still closed. The truth is, your brain doesn't fully believe the new story until you start living like it's true.

That's where intentional action comes in. Not hustle. Not overperforming. Just clear, value-aligned actions repeated often enough to override the old, automatic ones. Research on behavioral reinforcement shows that repetition is what wires your brain for change. Not pep talks. Not affirmations shouted into the bathroom mirror. Repetition. Action. Follow through. That's what transforms mindset from a good idea into your new normal.

But let's be honest. Taking action sounds a lot easier than it actually feels. Especially when you're shifting something deep, like the belief that you're not enough, or the reflex to shrink in a room where you know you should lead. That's why so many "self-talk" techniques don't stick. You can say all the right things in the mirror and still fall right back into old patterns by lunchtime.

Greg Anderson, CEO of Allegiant Air, said it perfectly during a conversation we had: "Growth doesn't come from ease. It comes from action. The more action you take, the more capacity you build. You don't get used to pressure. You get stronger under it."

This chapter is about building the bridge between what you *believe* and what you *do*. It's the part of the MINDSET Framework where we stop theorizing and start moving. The brain doesn't care about your title. It cares about what's repeated. So, whether you're running a team or rewriting your personal narrative, the process is the same: Choose the action, take the step, and reinforce the mindset until it becomes second nature.

This is the second to last step in the MINDSET journey, and it's the one that separates people who *talk* about change from the ones who actually live it.

How Taking Action Rewires the Brain

When it comes to rewiring your mindset, insight gets the spotlight, but it's action that does the heavy lifting. You can't just think your way into a new identity. You have to act your way into it. Real transformation doesn't come from an epiphany in your journal. It happens when your behavior starts aligning with the belief you're working to build.

Yes, recognizing your thoughts and shifting your lens is essential. That lays the groundwork. But if mindset awareness is the foundation, action is the reinforcement. Without it, your brain has no reason to update the script. It just nods and says, "Nice idea... anyway, back to panic mode."

That's where **neuroplasticity** comes in. We've touched on it before, but here's a quick recap: your brain is changeable. Flexible. Adaptable. Every time you make an intentional choice that aligns with growth, especially when fear is screaming at you, you're literally carving a new neural path. And just like physically building muscles, rewiring takes repetition. One workout won't transform your body, but show up consistently, and you start becoming someone new. The same applies to mindset. One bold moment doesn't make you confident. But a pattern of courageous behavior? That rewires how you see yourself and how others see you, too.

If you want to lead with more confidence, compassion, or courage, don't wait until you feel those things. Start doing what someone with those traits would do. Speak up when your name gets mispronounced. Hold your ground when someone interrupts you. Send the email. Set the boundary. These might feel small, uncomfortable, or downright terrifying, but they're reps. And every rep sends your brain a memo: *This is who we are now.*

Here's the truth: Powerful mindset shifts without action are just poetic theories. Your brain doesn't shift based on language. It shifts based on lived proof. When belief meets behavior, the brain takes notice. Insight becomes evidence, growth becomes trackable, and over time, your actions speak louder than the doubts that used to run the show.

So, yes, action rewires the brain. But not just any action. It has to be the right kind. The kind that matches the future you're building. Let's talk about what that actually looks like.

How to Take the Right Kind of Action

By now, it's clear that action matters, but let's be even clearer: *Not all action is the right action.* Busyness is not the same as growth, and crossing things off a to-do list doesn't mean you're evolving. Sometimes it just means you're really good at avoiding the thing that actually needs to change.

The right kind of action isn't about doing more. It's about doing what aligns. Aligned action is strategic. It reinforces the identity you're building, not the one you're trying to outgrow. It's what shifts your behavior from reactive to intentional, so you're not just responding to pressure, you're leading with clarity.

Sometimes, the right action looks bolder, like initiating a tough conversation you've been avoiding. Sometimes it looks softer, like pausing to listen instead of jumping in to fix. Sometimes it's uncomfortable, like asking for help when your ego would rather go it alone. The right action isn't always dramatic, but it's always intentional, and it always moves you closer to the mindset you're trying to lock in.

Think of each aligned action as casting a vote. One vote for the confident version of you. One vote for the resilient, present, emotionally intelligent leader you're becoming. Your brain doesn't need a dramatic reinvention. It just needs consistent, directional input.

And let's not confuse "right" with "perfect." The right action isn't about nailing it every time. It's about showing up with integrity. Specificity helps here: Instead of saying, *I'm going to be more confident,* reframe it into something measurable like, *I'll speak up at least once in every team meeting.* That's clear. That's trackable. That tells your brain: This isn't a wish; it's a pattern.

Also, the right kind of action will often feel weird at first. That's not failure; it's data. You're stretching into a new zone, and your nervous system hasn't caught up yet. Growth rarely feels graceful when it's happening. But that discomfort? That's the cost of a resilient mindset. You don't get new results by staying in old patterns, and you don't get to rewrite your mindset without walking it out one bold, awkward step at a time.

This isn't about chasing perfect outcomes. It's about practicing better inputs. And the more you practice taking the right kind of action, the more natural those choices become until one day, they're not brave. They're just *you*.

Barriers to Action and How to Overcome Them

Even with the best intentions, taking consistent action can feel like walking through wet cement: every step slower, heavier, and strangely sticky. You've done the work. You've reframed the thought. You're motivated. So why does it still feel so hard to move? It's because every time you try to step forward, you bump into a barrier. Not a literal wall (though those would be easier to deal with). These are the invisible kind—the mental roadblocks, emotional speed bumps, and habit loops your brain has spent years rehearsing. But here's the thing: Barriers don't mean you're broken. They mean you're bumping into your edges. I love this saying: With every level comes a different devil. You overcame the last one, and you'll overcome this one too.

These internal and external blocks aren't random. They're patterned. Often, they're the exact same forces that shaped your old mindset, and now they're trying to keep you tethered to it. But with self-awareness and the right strategy, you can unhook from those defaults. That's why this part of the framework doesn't introduce something "new." It helps you circle back to everything you've already learned and apply it in real time.

The MINDSET Framework isn't a clean staircase. It's more like a spiral ramp. You'll revisit pieces of it as you level up. Triggers don't vanish just because you identified them, and self-doubt doesn't disappear because you reframed it once. This isn't failure; it's integration, and once you recognize the loop, you can start redirecting it.

So, let's talk about what's actually getting in the way. Sometimes it's fear in disguise, masked as perfectionism or procrastination. Sometimes it's fatigue pretending to be indecision. Sometimes it's an old survival strategy that worked once but is now completely misaligned with where you're going. And yes, sometimes it's just your nervous system asking, Are we really doing this new thing again? as it tries to lure you back into safety mode with the tempting buzz of familiar discomfort.

What matters most is that you name the barrier, not shame it. Avoiding action is rarely about laziness. It's about protection. Your brain is trying to keep you safe. It just hasn't gotten the memo that you're safe *and* ready to evolve.

Each time you notice the resistance and choose action anyway, especially action that's aligned with your values and goals, you're not just pushing past the barrier. You're retraining your system to expect success where it used to expect shutdown.

Sometimes, moving forward looks like momentum. Other times, it looks like pausing, reassessing, and trying again without the dramatic soundtrack. Either way, it still counts.

The MINDSET Framework is designed to work as a whole, not in isolation. That's why some steps might overlap or blend together. It's not a flaw. It's how real transformation works. With that in mind, here are five common barriers to action and how you can move through them.

Fear of Failure or Judgment

One of the sneakiest barriers to action is the fear of getting it wrong, especially if someone's watching. This fear doesn't always show up yelling. Sometimes it whispers: *Let's tweak this one more time.* Or *Maybe next week when it's quieter.* Or my personal favorite: *Let's create a color coded spreadsheet first.*

Let's call it what it is: fear of judgment dressed up as preparation.

This kind of fear loves to blend in with productivity, but it's actually just performance anxiety with better PR, and the longer you avoid action, the more your brain believes that playing it safe is the smart thing to do. Which it is, if you're trying to stay stuck.

How to Overcome It

Redefine failure as feedback, not a final verdict. Every action, whether it's flawless or a little messy, gives your brain something valuable: data. That's how learning works. That's how wiring works. The shift starts when you stop asking, *What if I mess up?* and start asking, *What will I learn either way?*

Then take the next brave step. Small ones, daily and intentionally.

According to author Darren Hardy in *The Compound Effect*, it's not the big, dramatic gestures that create real transformation. It's the tiny, repeated ones that stack over time. That's how confidence is built. That's how fear gets rewired.

Do one thing every day that makes your stomach flip a little. Ask the uncomfortable question. Hit send on the idea you've been sitting on. Stretch into discomfort on purpose, and let repetition reshape your response.

Growth doesn't come from perfection. It comes from presence. From motion. From trying again.

People respect forward motion far more than they admire hesitation. You won't win everyone, but when you show up, take risks, learn, and keep going, you start building something stronger than perfection: credibility.

And failure? It's not a flaw. It's not proof that you don't belong. It's evidence that you're actually in the game. So say the thing. Send the pitch. Raise your hand. You don't need perfect. You need proof. One imperfect action at a time.

Overwhelm or Lack of Clarity

Sometimes, inaction isn't laziness; it's confusion. When the path forward looks more like a dense fog than a clear road, your brain hits pause. It's easier to default to distraction or procrastination than to step into the unknown. Imagine staring at a whiteboard full of scribbles and feeling like the only logical response is to walk away and pretend you never saw it. That's overwhelm—a mental shutdown that keeps you stuck before you even start.

For leaders, this paralysis can stall the momentum of entire teams. The pressure to "get it right" can feel so crushing that you freeze. But here's the kicker: Overwhelm isn't a sign of failure; it's your brain's way of protecting you from chaos. It's wired to avoid that feeling, even if that means avoiding progress.

How to Overcome It

The secret weapon against overwhelm? Break it down; way down. Instead of aiming to "improve team culture," start with something concrete: Send one weekly appreciation email to a team member. Tiny, deliberate actions like these create clarity and build unstoppable momentum.

Use this simple question as your compass: *What's one thing I can do today that aligns with the mindset I want?* That question cuts through the noise and points you to your next move, no matter how small.

Old Habits and Automatic Responses

Our brains have a serious crush on the familiar, kind of like that one pair of sweatpants you refuse to give up, even when they're clearly past their prime. Those well-worn neural pathways are your brain's favorite comfort zone. Stepping outside of them triggers an internal "Nope, not today" from your survival instincts. It's not stubbornness. It's just your brain trying to save you from the terrifying unknown (also known as change).

How to Overcome It

The secret weapon against this resistance? Visual cues and gentle reminders. Slap a sticky note on your laptop. Schedule a calendar alert. Heck, tie a string around your finger if you have to; whatever it takes to keep your new habits top of mind. And when resistance raises its grumpy head, don't take it personally. It's just your brain's way of saying, *Whoa, you're really pushing me here.* That's a good sign. Growth doesn't happen in the comfort zone. It happens in the awkward, slightly uncomfortable stretch just beyond it.

External Pressure and Lack of Support

Sometimes external circumstances, tight deadlines, toxic environments, or unsupportive relationships can limit your ability to act with intention.

How to Overcome It

Focus on what you can control, and take small steps within your sphere of influence. Build a support system, even if it's just one trusted peer or mentor who encourages your growth. Advocate for boundaries where possible. When you commit to action that reflects your growth mindset, you gradually influence your environment too often more than you realize.

Inner Critic

That nagging voice inside your head? Yeah, the one that pipes up with, *Who do you think you are?* It's not your friend. It's your inner critic, a fear-based record stuck on repeat, ready to sabotage before you even take the first step. The inner critic doesn't just whisper doubts. It's the VIP gatekeeper of inaction.

How to Overcome It

The first move? Call it out. Label that voice for what it really is: conditioned fear, not fact. Remember from earlier chapters, naming thoughts creates distance and power. Then crank up the volume on your core values. If courage or growth is on your list, take action that reflects those values, regardless of the noise your critic tries to make.

One of the hardest lessons I've learned (and yes, it took way too long) is that confidence doesn't show up before action. It shows up *because* of action. And it's rarely the grand, spotlight stealing moments that build lasting confidence. It's the small wins. Those bite sized, manageable steps that quietly prove to your brain the process is working and you're moving forward.

So, what counts as a small win? It's any clear, achievable action that aligns with your new mindset. Maybe it's a quick, honest 10-minute check-in with a team member when your old script would have you stay distant. Maybe it's speaking up with a new idea, asking that question in a meeting, or simply choosing to pause before reacting. These micro moves break down overwhelming goals into something real you can do *today*, and they build momentum that compounds.

Momentum is powerful, and because trying to overhaul your entire belief system overnight is like trying to sprint a marathon (a total momentum killer), start with one limiting belief. Pick your biggest or most stubborn one, and challenge it with intentional action. If you believe, *I must always have the answers,* a small win might be saying, *I don't know, but I'll find out.* One act of honesty chips away at old narratives and strengthens a new, empowered foundation.

Small wins might feel insignificant, but they're far from it. Every time you act aligned with your growth mindset and see positive outcomes, you're stacking internal proof. You quiet the inner critic, hush self-doubt, and build confidence that's earned, not wished for. Over time, those wins add up into undeniable evidence that your new mindset isn't just a nice idea. It's your reality.

That's when the magic happens. You stop trying to be confident and start embodying confidence.

Action Ideas to Consider

Taking action is the crucial bridge between shifting your mindset and making real-world impact. Thinking differently is a great start, but if you don't *live* differently, the transformation stays theoretical. Even the smallest actions can reinforce new beliefs, build your confidence muscle, and send a crystal clear message to your brain: *Change is happening here.*

Scenario 1: You're Afraid of Criticism

- **Old mindset:** "If I ask for feedback, they'll point out my flaws."

- **New mindset:** "Feedback helps me grow."

- **Action:** Ask a team member or peer, "What's one thing I could improve in how I communicate or lead?" Write down their response without defensiveness. Reflect on it and take one step toward implementing it.

Scenario 2: You Always Do Everything Yourself

- **Old mindset:** "If I want it done right, I have to do it myself."

- **New mindset:** "Empowering others strengthens the team."

- **Action:** Choose one task this week to delegate. Explain the *why* behind the task and let go of micromanaging. Use this as a chance to build trust and recognize team members' strengths.

Scenario 3: You Avoid Difficult Conversations

- **Old mindset:** "I don't want to make things worse."

- **New mindset:** "Clear is kind, and discomfort leads to clarity."

- **Action:** Prepare and schedule a conversation you've been avoiding. Write down your key message ahead of time, approach it with empathy, and focus on shared solutions.

Scenario 4: You Doubt Your Leadership Value

- **Old mindset:** "I'm not experienced enough to contribute."

- **New mindset:** "My voice and ideas matter."

- **Action:** Speak up once in every meeting this week, even if it's just to ask a clarifying question or share appreciation. Notice how you feel afterward and how others respond.

Scenario 5: You're Stuck in Comparison Mode

- **Old mindset:** "They're doing better than me; I'm behind."

- **New mindset:** "My growth journey is unique."

- **Action:** Unfollow one account or limit one source of comparison that drains you. Instead, write down three recent wins, big or small, that reflect your resilience and effort.

Mindset Reflection

As we wrap up this chapter, taking a practical step right now matters more than ever. This exercise will help you pause, recognize how far you've come, and get intentional about the next move. Because growth isn't a destination; it's a series of small, deliberate steps that add up to lasting change.

So take a breath, take the step, and keep building the leadership mindset you're meant to lead with.

Step 1: Identify One Small Action

Take a moment to think about the mindset shift you're working on. Now ask yourself these two important questions:

1. What is one small, meaningful action that reflects this new belief?

2. What would it look like to live this out in my daily leadership?

Here are some examples:

1. If your new mindset is "I grow through feedback," your small action might be: "Ask one person for feedback each week."

2. If your new mindset is "Delegation strengthens the team," your action could be: "Delegate one task every Monday."

Tip: The action should be simple, doable, repeatable, and not a massive overhaul. Small steps win the race.

Step 2: Do it Regularly

Choose the rhythm that works best for your schedule and goal. Will you do it daily, weekly, or even hourly, if necessary?

- Daily: Write down one way I led with confidence today.

- Weekly: Share one piece of authentic encouragement with a team member.

- Hourly: Pause and take one mindful breath before responding to stress.

Tip: Set a reminder if needed or add it to your phone calendar to ensure you don't forget about it.

Step 3: Build It Into Your Routine

Repetition rewires the brain. The more often you follow through on this small action, the more natural it becomes and the more your brain reinforces the new pathway. Use this mini habit as your anchor, a signal to your brain that you're committed to the new mindset.

Some reflection questions that might help with this step:

- Where in my day can I consistently fit this in?

- How will I track my consistency?

- What might get in the way, and how will I navigate that?

Bonus Step: Use a Journal Reflection

At the end of each day or week, use a journal prompt to help you reflect. Here are a few journal reflections to get you started:

- Did I take my chosen action today?

- How did it feel?

- What did I notice about my mindset before and after?

- What's one way I can build on this tomorrow?

This small but powerful practice helps you integrate new beliefs into your leadership life, one intentional action at a time.

Chapter 10

T—Track Your Progress

Lead with scarcity, and you're always playing catch up. Shift to abundance, and suddenly opportunities are everywhere you look.

– Sally Allen

A couple of years ago, I had a wake-up call. My lifestyle was dragging me down like a bad Netflix series I couldn't stop watching. To be open and transparent, menopause will do that to you. I was overweight, constantly tired, and out of breath after what should have been easy hikes. And while I was physically struggling, the real damage was happening upstairs. I was drowning in negative self-talk and beating myself up, thinking things like *How could I let myself go like this?* Naturally, my first move was to do what any rational adult would do: Google "fastest way to lose weight." Because let's be honest, who doesn't want a magic wand?

However, I took a moment to pause. I identified the trigger behind the negative thoughts, named the pattern, questioned it, and shifted my perspective. Then I followed it up with action. Long story short, I realized the heaviness I was feeling wasn't really about how I looked. It was about how I felt. My energy was gone, my motivation was shot, and my identity didn't match the life I was living. That's when it hit me: Losing weight fast wasn't the solution. This wasn't about a number on a scale. It was about aligning my mindset with the kind of person I actually wanted to be: a healthy, energized woman living a sustainable lifestyle, not a crash dieter stuck on a loop of extremes.

I realized I wouldn't change my life just by chasing goals. Real change would come from shifting who I believed I was. It wasn't just about trying to lose weight. It was about becoming someone who prioritized health every day. That mindset shift changed everything. My actions started to align with my identity, not just my intentions, and that's when the transformation really began.

Here's the rub about the slow road: There's no instant gratification. We live in a "now now now" world, but progress on big goals, like health or mindset, often feels like watching paint dry or worse, like standing still. Leaders know this dance well. You're grinding away, following the right steps, but the mirror doesn't change overnight. Does that mean you're failing? Hell no. It means you need to zoom out and start tracking progress, not just the big wins, but the small, daily wins that keep you moving forward.

Tracking progress is the final step in the Mindset Framework and one of the most essential. Skipping it is exactly why mindset rewiring crashes and burns for so many.

Why Tracking Progress is Crucial

Without tracking, motivation tanks and momentum stalls. So let's talk about why tracking isn't just helpful. It's your best friend on this journey.

This humble habit is the secret weapon separating wishful thinkers from real changemakers.

When you track progress, you do more than mark a checkbox; you create a running scorecard for your brain to see, process, and believe your growth.

It transforms invisible internal shifts into concrete, measurable proof that rewiring your mindset is working. Here are four reasons why tracking progress is such a vital step for your success.

Motivation

Tracking progress is like your brain's personal hype squad, delivering little dopamine hits every time you log a win. Seeing those small victories, inch by inch or pound by pound, fuels momentum like espresso for your mindset. You stop guessing if your efforts matter because the proof is right in front of you.

When you're on a journey, celebrating each milestone keeps you hooked. Whether it's the first pound lost or fitting into old jeans, those small wins train your brain to crave progress. On tough days, a quick glance at your progress log can reignite your "why" and remind you that you're actually doing this.

It's a built-in motivation booster that turns the grind into a game. So keep your scoreboard visible. Your brain loves to win.

Identifying Areas for Improvement

Tracking progress isn't just a victory lap; it's your personalized GPS for course correction. Maybe a pesky trigger keeps popping up, or you notice a stubborn thought that refuses to budge. Instead of letting these reveal your "failures," see them as signposts. When I tracked my progress, Saturdays stood out as my kryptonite (hello, weekend pizza and Netflix binges). But catching that allowed me to pivot, setting up mini-strategies to handle those lazy days better. Tracking is like being a savvy hiker: You don't wait to be hopelessly lost; you check the trail markers and adjust. It lets you refine your approach in real time, so you keep moving forward without wandering off the path.

Positive Reinforcement

Every progress note you jot down is a pat on the back for your brain. This consistent feedback loop builds up confidence and rewires that nagging inner dialogue from *I can't* to *I am*. I felt this firsthand with every pound dropped and every step walked. It's not about perfection. It's about recognizing progress and celebrating it with genuine pride. Think of tracking as your personal cheerleader, encouraging you to keep going when the inner critic gets loud. Those small wins stack up, proving the change isn't theoretical; it's happening. And that feeling? It's addictive, inspiring you to keep showing up for yourself every day.

Evaluating Effectiveness

Tracking isn't just about ticking boxes; it's your personal strategy lab—like being a mad scientist, but for your mindset. Which tools are actually moving the needle? Are those pause and breathe moments helping you respond like a pro instead of react like a squirrel on espresso? Is journaling actually shifting your perspective or just giving you extra words to delete later? Evaluating effectiveness means you get to toss out the stuff that's not working (goodbye, useless habits!) and double down on what is. It's you, leading your own growth journey with curiosity and a dash of swagger. Tracking closes the loop, turning mindset change from a vague idea into something real you can brag about. Ultimately, it hands you the steering wheel so you're driving your mind, not just holding on for dear life.

When Something's Not Working

So, you've followed the plan, tracked your progress, and yet that stubborn, stubborn mindset still feels like a heavy weight. Trying to shift it is like dragging a donkey uphill that's decided to lie down halfway: stubborn, unmoving, and completely uninterested in your growth goals. No matter what angle you attack from, it just won't budge. Now what? Do you toss this book onto the dusty shelf with all the other self-help books that promised the world but delivered nada? Do you throw in the towel and declare yourself hopelessly stuck? Or maybe you just grit your teeth and keep hoping for a miracle?

Hold up. None of those are your best moves. When progress stalls, it's a golden opportunity to lean into resilience, yes, but also to get strategic. Because when something isn't working, it's a signal, not a stop sign, and like any good leader, you don't quit at the first bump. You regroup, recalibrate, and keep steering toward change.

Here are four essential things to remember when the plan hits a wall.

Identify Why and Repeat the Process

When your progress stalls, resist the urge to toss your efforts in the trash bin of "that didn't work." Instead, pause, reflect, and revisit the earlier stages of the MINDSET Framework. Did you really label that thought, or just slap on a sticky note? Did you dissect the belief fully, or just skim the surface like a distracted pool floater? Mindset rewiring isn't a one-and-done deal. It's more like troubleshooting your favorite gadget. You don't chuck it when it glitches; you pop it open, poke around, and try again with fresh eyes. Give the process another spin. You might just discover a missing piece you overlooked..

Don't Lose Hope

Change isn't a straight shot; it's more like a winding hike with unexpected detours, snack breaks, and yes, the occasional moment when you question why you signed up. Frustration is normal; hopelessness is optional. Your brain is essentially learning a brand-new language (mindset fluency, anyone?). Like building muscle or mastering the art of sourdough, it demands patience and practice. Hope isn't some cheesy motivational cliché. It's a mindset in itself, an openness to possibility that fuels resilience. Setbacks aren't roadblocks; they're course corrections. You're not back at square one; you're in a better spot than you think.

Adjust What You Did the First Time

If your first try fizzled, adjust. Maybe your action wasn't bold enough, or the new belief felt faker than a three-dollar bill. Experimentation is your secret weapon. If journaling didn't click, try a coach, a trusted friend, or heck, even a voice memo. If your values felt fuzzy, dust off that core values exercise and give it another go. Progress isn't perfection; it's refinement. Tweak, test, and keep tuning your approach.

Make Sure It's Personal

Surface-level mindset shifts are like quick fixes with duct tape; they won't hold up under pressure. The real work happens when your new belief is as personal as your favorite coffee order. Use the Five Whys method to dig deep and ask *why* until you hit the raw core beneath the fear or doubt. If your thought is, *I'll never be a confident leader,* keep peeling back those layers until you uncover the real story. The deeper the roots, the stronger the growth. Don't stop until your mindset shift is wired into your very identity, and you're no longer running someone else's script, but your own.

How to Track Progress

By now, we can all agree that tracking progress isn't optional. It's essential. But that leads to the million-dollar question: *How?* Tracking your progress doesn't have to feel like rocket science, but it absolutely must be intentional. The goal is to build a system that gives you clear visibility into your mindset journey: what's working, what's stumbling, and how far you've come. When done right, tracking becomes your secret weapon, fueling motivation, sharpening self-awareness, and reinforcing the mindset you're working hard to build. It's less about perfect spreadsheets and more about honest reflection and measurable action.

So, how do you get started? Here are a few practical, no-fluff strategies to keep your mindset transformation on track, because progress that's tracked is progress that sticks.

Mindset Journal

I've spoken about journals a couple of times already because they really work. A dedicated journal used specifically to track your progress can be incredibly helpful. It's like a little logbook but for your mind. Each day or week, write down your thoughts, wins, or challenges to keep a clear record of your mindset journey.

For those who don't love writing, digital journals offer a great alternative. You can leave voice notes or use voice-to-text features to capture your reflections. This flexibility makes it easier to stay consistent and keeps the tracking process approachable, even on your busiest days.

Each day or week, you write down:

- The triggers you've experienced.
- The thoughts you've labelled and dissected.
- New perspectives you tried.
- Actions you took.
- How you felt afterward.

This kind of reflective journaling helps you connect the dots and notice patterns over time. It's also powerful to flip back through your entries and see how your mindset has shifted.

Weekly Self-Check-In

Create a habit of checking in with yourself at the end of each week. Ask yourself:

- What wins did I experience this week?
- What challenged me?
- Did I notice any recurring thoughts or triggers?
- How did I respond differently than I might have in the past?

- What action did I take that felt aligned with my values?

Write these reflections down or use them as part of a voice note or video log, if that suits you better.

Progress Tracker

Use a simple spreadsheet, app, or habit tracker to monitor consistent actions that support your mindset shift. For example:

- Practiced pause
- Labelled a thought
- Dissected a belief
- Took aligned action
- Tracked progress

Seeing those checkmarks add up is a visual reminder that you are doing the work even when it feels slow.

Monthly Reflection

At the end of each month, take time to reflect more broadly:

- What beliefs have changed?
- How am I thinking or responding differently now?
- How has my leadership been impacted?
- Where do I still feel stuck?

You can even write a letter to your future self, summarizing where you are now and where you want to be a month from now.

Feedback From Others

Sometimes, we're so close to our own mindset shifts that we don't see the progress happening. That's where a trusted colleague, coach, or team member can step in and offer fresh eyes. Ask them questions like:

- Have you noticed any changes in how I handle challenges?

- Do I seem more open or flexible lately?

- What's something I've done recently that really stood out to you?

Getting feedback from others can be a powerful reality check. It confirms that all the internal work you're doing is actually showing up in the real world and that your mindset shifts aren't just good intentions but real results.

Mindset Wins Board

This could be a digital board (think Trello or Notion) or a physical space on your wall where you collect your mindset wins. Sticky notes, screenshots, feedback messages, or quotes, anything that shows your growth and progress. When the going gets tough, this board turns into your personal victory dance floor, reminding you just how far you've come.

The tool itself doesn't matter as much as your commitment to consistency and honesty. Tracking your mindset journey this way keeps you grounded and proves something important: Change isn't just a vague idea. It's real, it's measurable, and it's happening every single step of the way.

Mindset Reflection

To make tracking your progress a bit more fun and way less like a chore, try this simple weekly activity. Set aside just 10 minutes at the end of your week to reflect and jot down your thoughts in your journal. No pressure, no judgment, just honest answers to a few straightforward questions. Think of it as your personal check-in with yourself to see how far you've come.

1. **What's one mindset shift I noticed in myself this week?** Big or small, it all counts. Maybe you paused before reacting, asked for feedback, or responded with curiosity instead of judgment.

2. **What action did I take that aligned with my resilient mindset?** Did you speak up in a meeting? Reframe a limiting belief? Delegate more confidently?

3. **What's one area I'd like to improve next week?** Maybe it's pausing more often, labelling thoughts more clearly, or leaning into discomfort with courage.

Bonus Tip: Keep your weekly snapshots together in a single place so you can review them monthly. Over time, you'll build a powerful narrative of transformation and progress.

Section 3: The Success

A transformed mindset isn't a destination;
it's the lens through which you see and shape your world.

– Sally Allen

You've journeyed through the MINDSET Framework step by step, insight by insight, and now you've reached a powerful turning point. You've learned how to pause, spot your triggers, name those pesky thoughts, dissect stubborn beliefs, shift your perspective, take action, and track your progress. Not too shabby, right? This isn't small potatoes! It takes guts, grit, and a willingness to do the inner work most people avoid (while binge watching Hulu).

But here's the million-dollar question: What happens *next*?

This final section is all about locking in your success and building the kind of resilience that sticks around long after you close this book. Because let's face it, transformation doesn't happen in a neat little bubble or on a PowerPoint slide. It shows up in the glorious chaos of real life: the messy, beautiful, unpredictable dance of leadership and day-to-day living. *The Success* is about the "after." After the motivation fades, after your shiny new mindset gets thrown in the ring with real-world challenges, and after those pesky setbacks threaten to drag you back to old habits faster than you can say "comfort zone." This section is your survival guide for staying power.

You'll find two chapters here: One prepares you for setbacks (spoiler: they're coming, so get ready), and the other dives into continuous implementation—how to make mindset work part of your daily groove, not just a one-time miracle.

Think of this as your launchpad. The earlier chapters gave you the tools, but now it's time to make those tools part of your DNA. Because rewiring your mindset isn't about one glorious "aha" moment; it's about the daily choices, the constant self-check-ins, and the long game that separates leaders who evolve from those stuck in last season's reruns.

Let's finish strong. Let's make sure your mindset transformation is more than a chapter. Let's make sure it's the headline act of your leadership story.

I mean, honestly, wouldn't you rather be the leader/individual who's always upgrading than the one stuck buffering in the background?

Chapter 11

Preparing for Setbacks

*The way you handle setbacks will define your
leadership more than the way you handle success.*

– Sally Allen

I've got something important to tell you, something I wish someone had
handed me on a silver platter years ago. Here it is: Setbacks are not just
normal; they're inevitable. If you think you'll close this book with a "perfect"
mindset, you're setting yourself up for frustration and disappointment.

Self-help culture often sells us this fantasy: Read the last chapter, and *bam*,
problem solved. But real transformation? It's just getting started. Setbacks
will show up, uninvited and relentless. So why bother trying if failure seems
certain? Because failure and setbacks aren't the same thing.

Picture this: There's an obstacle blocking your path. Failure is when you
quit. A setback? That's when you get rejected or beaten down, but you dust
yourself off and get back up.

It took me years to truly shift my mindset and accept what I now call a
Sally-ism: "Life is always 'lifeing.'" You don't get to go around the storm;

you have to go through it." Over time, you learn to hold both the good and the bad because they come as a package deal. I had to get ready for people to be, well... people. To let me down. To disappoint me. I had to prepare to lose loved ones, to fall flat on my face, to fail hard, and then find the strength to stand back up again.

That's the grit of leadership and life, normalizing setbacks frees you from the crushing weight of perfectionism and the myth that progress is a straight line. When your team sees you handle setbacks with calm confidence, they learn resilience too. That's how a growth mindset spreads beyond you and takes root.

In this chapter, we'll explore the nature of setbacks and how to prepare for them. Because the goal isn't to dodge every curveball, you can't, but to equip yourself with the tools to hit them out of the park.

Understanding the Nature of Setbacks

Setbacks aren't the villain in your story. They're just part of the plot twists. Anyone chasing meaningful change will face them. The journey to a stronger mindset isn't a straight line; it's a rollercoaster with loops, sharp turns, and occasional nausea. If you expect smooth sailing, you're in for a surprise.

The trick? Stop treating setbacks like personal flaws or evidence that you're "not enough." Instead, see them as natural speed bumps. They're annoying, sure, but also useful. They force you to slow down, check your map, and sometimes take a different route. Setbacks show up in all shapes and sizes: a conversation gone sideways, a goal missed, a day when your motivation evaporates. They test your resolve and your capacity to keep moving forward despite discomfort. But here's the game changer: Setbacks aren't permanent roadblocks. They're invitations to pivot and learn. They're reality checks, yes, but also opportunities to flex your leadership muscles and deepen your self-awareness. So next time you hit a snag, don't throw in the towel. Lean in. Ask yourself what the setback is teaching you. What needs adjustment? What strengths can you call on?

Because setbacks don't define you; they refine you. Resilience isn't bouncing back perfectly; it's bouncing back with purpose. Your mindset isn't about flawless progress; it's about relentless growth.

Dealing With Setbacks

Knowing setbacks are coming is only half the battle. Actually being ready for them is the real win. When you've got the right mindset and tools in your toolkit, setbacks lose their power to knock you off course. Instead, they become challenges you face head-on with confidence and clarity.

Think of these tools as your mental toolkit, reliable and ready whenever life decides to throw a curveball. They help you reframe tough moments, regroup your energy, and rise stronger than before. No more flailing or panic mode; just steady, strategic moves that keep your momentum alive.

The following tools are like a mental toolkit available to you whenever you need them, helping you reframe, regroup, and rise stronger.

"Lemonading:" Reframing With a Playful Mindset

When life hands you lemons, don't just make lemonade, make a whole darn lemon festival. This playful phrase is more than a cliché. It's a resilience strategy I call "lemonading." It's the mindset of looking at a frustrating, disappointing, or painful situation and asking, *How can I turn this around? What good can come from this mess?* It doesn't mean ignoring the bitter parts. It means using them.

This isn't about toxic positivity or plastering on a fake smile. It's about choosing curiosity and creativity over defeat and despair. Leaders who get good at lemonading can spin missed opportunities into fresh ideas, failures into lessons, and slammed doors into new pathways. Make lemonading a habit, and setbacks stop feeling like dead ends. Instead, they become the gritty, raw ingredients you use to cook up your next big win.

Look at Your Track Record

Look, you've been through the wringer before, and guess what? You're still standing. That's no small thing. When setbacks hit, one of the smartest moves is to hit the rewind button and analyze your past experiences. What went down? How did it make you feel? What tools or mindset shifts helped you claw your way forward? What lessons did you pocket?

In the heat of a tough moment, it's easy to forget just how tough you really are. But your history? It's packed with proof of your grit and resilience. By mining those past wins and hard-earned lessons, you're arming yourself with a battle-tested playbook. That wisdom doesn't just sit on a shelf; it guides your next moves with confidence and clarity.

Adjusting Strategies

When a setback hits, the smartest move isn't to toss the whole plan out the window. Often, the foundation is solid, it just needs a different angle or a bit of tweaking. Flexibility is the secret sauce of a resilient mindset and leadership.

If your plan's sputtering, that doesn't mean you're slacking. It means it's time to shift gears. Maybe you need to tweak the timeline, recalibrate your goals, delegate differently, or simply reframe your expectations.

Think of setbacks as your personal "adjustment alerts," not as full system shutdowns. The difference? One keeps you moving forward with finesse, the other leaves you stuck spinning your wheels. Pivot smartly, lead boldly, and watch how setbacks become setups for your next win.

Self-Care Practices

Setbacks have a sneaky way of draining you emotionally, mentally, and sometimes physically, like a phone left on 1% without a charger in sight.

That's why the basics aren't basic; they're critical. Rest, restore, reconnect. Self-care isn't a luxury reserved for spa days; it's your lifeline in the chaos.

Whether it's meditation, deep breathing, a walk in nature, a power nap, or indulging in your favorite hobby (yes, even binge reading or cooking counts), these practices pull you back to center. When your internal battery is fully charged, you don't just survive the storm; you navigate it with energy and clarity.

Self-care isn't about erasing challenges; it's about building resilience to respond instead of react. And here's the kicker: When self-care becomes part of your everyday leadership routine, setbacks don't catch you off guard. You're ready, you're steady, and you lead with intention, not panic.

Mindset Reflection

Setbacks lose their grip when you've got a plan. Instead of scrambling like a headless chicken when challenges pop up, imagine having a go-to routine, a personalized reset button that helps you pause, regroup, and move forward with purpose.

This activity is designed to help you build that routine, so next time life throws a curveball, you're not caught flat-footed. Take 10 to 15 minutes to work through the prompts below. Think of it as your "Setback Safety Net," a simple, reliable plan you can pull out anytime you feel off balance.

Because let's be honest: Winging it rarely works, but with a little preparation, setbacks become just another step on your path to leadership greatness.

- Step 1: **What typically throws you off?** Think back to recent setbacks. What kind of situations tend to trigger stress or discouragement for you? Example: Missing a deadline, receiving critical feedback, a team conflict, low energy, or burnout.

- Step 2: What helps you reset and ground yourself? List three to five actions that help you feel calm, re-centered, or uplifted. These can be small habits or rituals; things that remind you of your strength and help you reset your mindset. Example: Go for a walk, talk to a mentor, journal for five minutes, meditate, or re-read past wins or encouragements.

- Step 3: **What new mindset or phrase do you want to remember during setbacks?** Choose a phrase, mantra, or belief that can act as your anchor when things go wrong. Something simple, empowering, and true. Example: "This is a setup, not a stop."

- Step 4: Build Your Routine. Now, combine your answers into a simple Setback Routine: a short list you can refer to the moment you feel stuck or discouraged. For example:

  o Pause and breathe

  o Remind myself

  o Do one reset action

  o Reflect

  o Adjust my plan if needed

- **Bonus step:** Write or print your routine and keep it somewhere visible on your desk, in your planner, or as a note in your phone. The more you practice it, the more automatic it becomes.

Chapter 12

Continuous Implementation

Leadership begins the moment you stop fearing discomfort and start embracing change.

– Sally Allen

Do you know the difference between a mediocre leader and a great one? A great leader keeps showing up, especially when it's hard or inconvenient. When others freeze, they move. When the outcome is uncertain, they still lead. That's the difference. It's not perfection. It's persistence. I'm incredibly fortunate to be the leader and coach I am today because of leaders who modeled that kind of resilience. Their continued mentorship has shaped the way I show up, push forward, and lead with purpose.

And here we are, at the final step of our journey and it's arguably the most important: *continuous implementation.* I'll say it loud and clear: Rewiring your mindset isn't a one-and-done deal. It's not a weekend workshop or a motivational binge-watch. It's consistent, daily effort and commitment to showing up for yourself and your leadership every single day.

All the brilliant insights you've gathered from this book and your career are worthless if they don't make it into your daily routine. Change doesn't stick without action that's steady and intentional. Consistency is your secret weapon, and positive habits are the backbone that makes that weapon unstoppable.

In this brief but powerful chapter, we'll unpack why consistency is king, how habit formation propels mindset rewiring, and how to embrace an infinite, evolving leadership mindset.

So let's close this book not with a whisper, but with a loud roar that is resilient, ready, and relentless.

Real transformation demands consistent practice. Think of it this way: hitting the gym once won't turn you into a muscle-bound superhero overnight, and rewiring your brain won't stick after one journaling session or a single courageous conversation. I have said this over and over again: Consistency is the quiet, relentless force that turns insights into action and action into identity.

You might not feel the shift immediately. Heck, the changes might feel invisible at first, especially when no one's watching. But every day you practice, whether it's journaling, reframing, pausing to breathe, or simply practicing awareness—you're paving new mental highways. Those "this is just who I am" beliefs? They start to fade like bad wallpaper. Meanwhile, your fresh, empowered beliefs take root and grow stronger.

Here's a metaphor: Brushing your teeth takes minutes a day, but that tiny habit keeps your smile healthy for decades. Mindset hygiene works the same way. Spending a few intentional minutes daily can compound into profound change over time.

So don't wait for the dramatic leaps. Forget the flashy breakthroughs. The secret weapon is simple: Keep stepping forward, day after day. That's how leaders build resilience, rewrite their stories, and transform not just their mindset but their lives.

Habit Formation and Reinforcement

Every habit follows a simple but powerful loop: cue, routine, and reward. This cycle is the engine that turns conscious effort into automatic behavior. When rewiring your mindset, you'll go through this loop again and again until this way of thinking isn't just something you do; it becomes who you are. Let's break it down.

- **Cue:** The trigger that kicks off your behavior (think stress hitting you like a freight train).

- **Routine:** The behavior itself (pausing to breathe instead of knee-jerk reacting).

- **Reward:** The payoff you get (feeling calm, proud, and in control).

To build new mental habits, start by spotting the cues that ignite your old mindset and consciously swap in a fresh routine. Say your trigger is unexpected critical feedback. Your default might be to get defensive, clam up, or spiral into self-doubt. Instead, hit pause, breathe, remind yourself of your worth, and seek clarity. Your reward? A response that builds your confidence and strengthens relationships.

Solidify these new thought patterns with the tools we've covered: journaling, affirmations, or accountability partners. And here's the secret: It's not about perfection. Habit formation is messy and non-linear. You stumbled? That's totally fine! What counts is that you get back on the horse, again and again.

The Role of Environment and Community

Inner work is crucial, but don't underestimate the power of your external environment. It can either fuel your transformation or drain your progress faster than a bad Wi-Fi connection. There's a nugget of truth in the saying, "You are the sum of the five people you hang out with." So, if you're hanging around complainers who turn every challenge into a doom-and-gloom forecast, good luck staying motivated.

On the flip side, surrounding yourself with people who stretch you, support you, and share your values of resilience and growth is like giving your mindset rocket fuel. Your progress won't just happen; it'll accelerate.

So, here's the real question: Who's in your corner?

Start by identifying one or two trusted people, a mentor, coach, colleague, or friend who you can check in with regularly. Better yet, join communities that champion continuous growth such as mastermind groups, leadership cohorts, or professional forums. Dive into books, podcasts, and conversations that challenge your thinking and keep you sharp.

Your environment should be a garden that nourishes your mindset, not a desert that dries it up. And don't forget to be that supportive person for others. When you model resilience and growth, you give your team and your organization permission to do the same.

Transformation isn't just a solo journey; it's contagious. Change yourself, and you ripple out, influencing your world one conversation, one decision, and one mindset shift at a time.

The Infinite Resilient Mindset

I've said this many times, and I'll say it again: Mindset transformation is lifelong. It's less a sprint and more an endless marathon with unexpected hills, rest stops, and surprise detours. As you grow, new challenges pop up, old patterns sneak back in wearing new disguises, and you hit ceilings you didn't even see coming. As I said before, "With every level comes a new devil." But here's the kicker: That's not failure. That's you being human.

The goal isn't to become some flawless, mindset guru who's got it all figured out. The real win is staying curious, asking tough questions, and committing to the daily practice of growth. Resilient leaders aren't those who've "arrived." They're the ones who've embraced the grind and made peace with being a work in progress.

So when you hit a wall, feel stuck, or the mental fog rolls in, don't freak out. Remember your toolkit: Pause, identify the trigger, name the thought, dissect it, shift your perspective, engage in action, and track your progress. Then rinse and repeat.

Mindset Reflection

As we wrap up this journey, here's a powerful exercise to seal your mindset transformation: a letter to your future self. Take a moment to put pen to paper (or fingers to keyboard) and write a note filled with gratitude and encouragement. Reflect on the key insights you've gained, the moments that truly resonated, and most importantly, your *why*—why you're committed to this mindset shift.

Write to yourself as you would to a close friend or a sibling: kind, honest, and full of compassion. Celebrate your progress, no matter how small it feels right now. Remind yourself of your strength and resilience. This isn't just a feel-good exercise; it's a strategic move to build your internal support system.

Once written, tuck that letter somewhere safe, but don't bury it so deep that even Indiana Jones couldn't find it. This letter is your future insurance policy. When setbacks shake your confidence or the change feels slow, pull it out. Let your own words remind you why you started and why you'll keep going.

You've done the work. You've got this. Now, write the letter that keeps you moving forward because sometimes the most powerful motivation comes from the voice you already carry inside. You got this.

Your mindset feels like a private affair—your own internal playlist—but as a leader, it's actually more like a stadium concert everyone's attending. How you respond under pressure, treat your team, and handle failure is on full display, whether you like it or not. Over time, your mindset doesn't just stay personal; it *creates* the culture around you.

Approach challenges with curiosity and calm, and your team will pick up that vibe like a catchy tune. React with fear and rigidity, and guess what? They'll follow that beat too. Your mindset is a ripple machine; spread it well, and it can either build a powerhouse team or a sinking ship.

If your mindset is stuck in negative territory, you're leading toward low trust, poor communication, burnout, and a blame game that's about as fun as a root canal. But a positive mindset? That's your ticket to higher morale, motivation, collaboration, and resilience that can weather any storm.

Remember, how you think sets the emotional thermostat for your whole team, which directly impacts their performance.

Scary thought? Maybe. Especially if you're feeling overwhelmed or carrying guilt over leading with a rigid mindset. Here's a quick reset: Take a deep breath. Breathe out the guilt, breathe in the determination. Change is coming, and it starts with you.

Conclusion

We have come full circle, and it's appropriate to end the way we started.

Most little girls wish for ponies or princess dresses when they turn eight.

I wished I could die.

To fade away into the background, away from pain, fear, and uncertainty. But today, I'm still here. I'm stronger, wiser, and more resilient than I ever imagined possible, and I still have ways to go. Every hard moment, every trial that almost broke me, became the soil where my mindset of resilience, tenacity, and adaptability took root and grew. The road was anything but easy. Sometimes it was rocky, and it was often steep, but looking back now, I smile because every step, every stumble, every victory has led me here: to this moment, right now, with you.

If you're reading these words, pause for a moment. Take a deep breath in and out. You've made it. Not just to the end of this book, but through a transformative journey of reflection, challenge, and growth. That is no small feat. You've explored what mindset truly means and how it shapes your life, your leadership, and your legacy. You've confronted your inner dialogue, faced discomfort, and tackled the MINDSET framework head-on, pausing, identifying, naming, dissecting, shifting, engaging, and tracking. Each step demanded courage, self-awareness, and an unwavering willingness to grow. That is leadership in its purest form.

Here's the honest truth: This isn't the finish line. Far from it. This is your launchpad. Your mindset journey is not about arriving at some mythical state of perfection; it's about committing to the process, day after day, choice after choice. It's about persistence. Keep choosing growth over fear. Whenever life tests you, and it will, lean on the tools you've built here. You're equipped now. You've planted seeds in your mind, seeds that, with care and consistency, will bloom into confidence, clarity, and resilience.

What's next? Live it. Lead with it. Let this mindset permeate your team meetings, your toughest decisions, your quietest moments, and your boldest dreams. Become the kind of leader who doesn't just transform herself or himself but ignites transformation in others. Because real leadership is contagious.

And if this book has sparked even a flicker of change in you, I ask one thing: Take a moment to share your experience in a review. Your voice helps others find this path. It keeps this work alive, growing, and evolving just like you.

Thank you for trusting me to walk alongside you on this journey. Here's to your next chapter as a rewired, resilient, and unstoppable leader. The journey forward? It's all yours.

The M.I.N.D.S.E.T. Framework: Your Recap

Every great leader knows that clarity beats chaos. So let's bring it all home. This framework is not just theory, it is your practical toolkit for rewiring your thoughts, leading with intention, and building a mindset that holds up under pressure.

M – Move to Pause

The pause is your power button. Stop, breathe, and create the mental space you need before reacting. Think of it as saving yourself from sending that email you would regret five minutes later.

I – Identify the Trigger

What set you off? Do not just feel the reaction, trace it back. Your boss's tone? That look from your colleague? Or maybe it was just the printer jamming again. Naming it gives you back the steering wheel.

N – Name the Thought

Call the thought what it is: fear, doubt, judgment, assumption. Once you label it, you separate yourself from it. You are not your thought; you are just temporarily hosting it like a bad Airbnb guest.

D – Dissect the Belief

Ask if the belief is true, helpful, or aligned with who you want to be. Spoiler alert: "I'm terrible at this" usually does not hold up under cross-examination.

S – Shift Your Perspective

Swap the lens. Reframe the challenge into an opportunity, the obstacle into feedback, the failure into data. It is like putting on new glasses and suddenly the blur makes sense.

E – Engage in Action

New mindset meets new behavior. Action is where rewiring sticks. Even one small step counts. Think less "climb Everest tomorrow" and more "maybe just lace up the sneakers today."

T – Track Your Progress

Growth leaves clues. Write it down, measure it, celebrate it. Because let's be honest, if you do not celebrate the small wins, your brain will keep waiting for the confetti cannon that never comes.

This is the framework. Simple, powerful, and repeatable. If you use this framework, you can change your mindset and change your life. Mindset mastered. Success inevitable.

About the Author, Sally Allen

Sally Allen is an award winning Executive Coach, Leadership Development Consultant, Author, and Podcaster with 25 years of corporate experience. She helps executives and teams shift the way they think so they can lead with greater clarity, connection, and impact. Known for her down-to-earth, results-driven style, Sally partners with organizations to build high-performing teams that thrive on trust, communication, and accountability.

Sally is the recipient of the 2025 Stevie Women in Business Award and the 2025 Stevie Best Entrepreneur - Business & Professional Services Award.

Her expertise spans both large corporations and small businesses, tackling challenges such as change management, team misalignment, low morale, confidence gaps, and communication breakdowns. At the heart of her coaching is her signature M.I.N.D.S.E.T. Framework, a research-backed model that rewires how leaders think, lead, and show up. Through this framework, Sally equips leaders with practical tools to strengthen culture, inspire performance, and navigate tough conversations with confidence and courage.

Beyond her coaching work, Sally serves as Chapter President of the International Association of Women (IAW) in Las Vegas (2024-2026), where she champions opportunities for women to grow, lead, and connect. She is equally passionate about philanthropic efforts that create lasting community impact.

When she's not coaching, speaking, or writing, you'll find her behind the mic on her podcast, sharing mindset strategies and exploring the realities of leadership. At home, she's "dog mom" to Max and Loki, her loyal sidekicks who keep her grounded and laughing.

If your goal is to develop confident leaders, strengthen team performance, and create a culture where people actually want to show up and contribute, Sally and her proven M.I.N.D.S.E.T. Framework are the partners you want in your corner.

References

Balban, M. Y., Neri, E., Kogon, M. M., Weed, L., Nouriani, B., Jo, B., Holl, G., Zeitzer, J. M., Spiegel, D., & Huberman, A. D. (2023). Brief structured respiration practices enhance mood and reduce physiological arousal. Cell Reports Medicine, 4(1), 1–15. https://doi.org/10.1016/j.xcrm.2022.100895

Barsade, S., & O'Neill, O. (2016, November 17). Manage your emotional culture. Harvard Business Review. https://hbr.org/2016/01/manage-your-emotional-culture

Bechara, A., Damasio, H., & Damasio, A. R. (2000). Emotion, decision making and the orbitofrontal cortex. Cerebral Cortex, 10(3), 295–307. https://doi.org/10.1093/cercor/10.3.295

Brené Brown, *Daring Greatly: How the Courage to Be Vulnerable Transforms the Way We Live, Love, Parent, and Lead* (New York: Gotham Books, 2012).

Clear, J. (2018). Atomic habits: An easy & proven way to build good habits & break bad ones. Penguin Publishing Group.

Dweck, Carol S. (2007). Mindset: The New Psychology of Success. Ballantine Books.

Emmons, R. A., & McCullough, M. E. (2003). Counting blessings versus burdens: An experimental investigation of gratitude and subjective well-being in daily life. Journal of Personality and Social Psychology, 84(2), 377–389. https://doi.org/10.1037/0022-3514.84.2.377

Feldman, L. (2018). How emotions are made: The secret life of the brain. Mariner Books.

Festinger, L. (1957). A theory of cognitive dissonance. Stanford University Press.

Fogg, B. J. (2019). Tiny habits : The small changes that change everything. Houghton Mifflin Harcourt.

Goldman, B. (2017, March 30). Study shows how slow breathing induces tranquility. Stanford Medicine. https://med.stanford.edu/news/all-news/2017/03/study-discovers-how-slow-breathing-induces-tranquility.html

Goleman, D. (1995). Emotional intelligence: Why it can matter more than IQ. Bloomsbury.

Gross, J. J. (1998). The emerging field of emotion regulation: An integrative review. Review of General Psychology, 2(3), 271–299. https://doi.org/10.1037/1089-2680.2.3.271

Hardy, D. (2010). *The Compound Effect*. New York: Vanguard Press.

Hayes, S. C., Strosahl, K. D., & Wilson, K. G. (1999). Acceptance and Commitment Therapy: An experiential approach to behavior change. New Harbinger Publications.

Kabat-Zinn, J. (1990). Full catastrophe living: Using the wisdom of your body and mind to face stress, pain, and illness. New York Dell Publishing Co.

Lazarus, R. S., & Folkman, S. (1984). Stress, appraisal, and Coping. Springer Publishing Company.

Ledoux, J. E. (1996). The emotional brain: The mysterious underpinnings of emotional life. Simon & Schuster.

Lyubomirsky, S. (2008). The how of happiness : A practical guide to getting the life you want. Penguin Press.

Merriam-Webster. (n.d.). Definition of mindset. Merriam-Webster. https://www.merriam-webster.com/dictionary/mindset

Novak, S. (2021, April 15). Fight or Flight? Why Our Caveman Brains Keep Getting Confused. Discover Magazine. https://www.discovermagazine.com/health/fight-or-flight-why-our-caveman-brains-keep-getting-confused

Rodríguez, G. S. (2021, January 25). Defusion: How to detangle from thoughts & feelings. The Psychology Group Fort Lauderdale. https://thepsychologygroup.com/defusion/

Segal, Z. V., Williams, J. M. G., & Teasdale, J. D. (2002). Mindfulness-based cognitive therapy for depression: A new approach to preventing relapse. Guilford Press.

Schacter, D. L., Addis, D. R., & Buckner, R. L. (2007). Remembering the past to imagine the future: The prospective brain. Nature Reviews Neuroscience, 8(9), 657–661. https://doi.org/10.1038/nrn2213

Toyota. (2025). Toyota production system. Toyota Motor Corporation Official Global Website. https://global.toyota/en/company/vision-and-philosophy/production-system/

www.ingramcontent.com/pod-product-compliance
Lightning Source LLC
Chambersburg PA
CBHW031319120626
46554CB00001BA/471